KEEP IT SIMPLE WITH

GarageBand

EASY MUSIC PROJECTS FOR BEGINNERS

Keith Gemmell

PC Publishing

PC Publishing
Keeper's House
Merton
Thetford
Norfolk IP25 6QH
UK

Tel +44 (0)1953 889900
Fax +44 (0)1953 889901
email info@pc-publishing.com
website http://www.pc-publishing.com

First published 2006

ISBN 1 870775 163

British Library Cataloguing in Publication Data
A catalogue record for this book is available from the British Library

Cover design by Hilary Norman Design Ltd

Printed and bound in Great Britain by Biddles, Kings Lynn, Norfolk

Contents

Introduction

Let's face it, for many beginners and amateur musicians new to computer-based music making, much of today's top-of-the-range recording software is far too complicated to operate. And believe me, that goes for many a professional musician and composer too.

Now I'm no musical technophobe but I've lost count of the times I've started my working day full of ideas and creative enthusiasm only to finish it exasperated and musically unfulfilled. Why? Because I'd spent hours with top of the range audio software suites, fiddling with EQ, tweaking effects, quantising notes, un-quantising notes and generally going round in circles. Instead of squandering valuable time in the pursuit of sonic perfection, what I should have been doing was recording new ideas, quickly and efficiently, while they were still fresh and exciting. 'Bring back the days of the simple analogue tape recorder', you might have heard me scream.

When sequencers like Cubase and Logic first appeared they were MIDI only applications, used to control synthesisers and drum machines. The actual sounds of these instruments, the audio output, were recorded onto analogue tape, alongside the acoustic instruments and vocals. But as these applications evolved and digital audio became an affordable reality, the sequencer took over the task of recording the audio content as well. Although incredibly convenient, this new technology has become increasingly complex to use especially for the beginner. Instead of helping musicians capture their musical inspirations quickly, these programs often have the opposite effect and sometimes even stifle their creativity.

And then, along came GarageBand. At last a simple, easy-to-use audio and MIDI sequencer for the masses; something everybody could use, amateurs and pros alike; the software equivalent of the old-fashioned tape recorder, only much more powerful.

You see, with GarageBand, the complicated stuff remains hidden from view, with just the basic controls on display. The interface is friendly and inviting rather than off-putting and capturing your ideas is quick and intuitive. And that got me thinking. I'd already written project books for some of the more expensive audio software suites. It's about time, I decided, to write a project book to accompany GarageBand.

And here it is: *Keep it Simple with GarageBand*, a series of 10 easy music-making projects written specifically for beginners and amateur musicians. Follow these simple projects and you'll not only learn how to use GarageBand effectively, you'll also pick up tons of insider tips on music making, constructing tunes and pro-style audio production along the way, all explained in easy-to-understand terminology.

About the projects

Apart from project 1, which deals with the very important subject of time and tempo, each individual project is a step towards the completion of a greater whole; a short jingle and voice-over track entitled, appropriately enough, *Keep It Simple With GarageBand*.

Any amateur musician can do these projects. You start by constructing a rhythm section with Apple loops, add a horn section, and learn simple editing tricks. Later you learn to record GarageBand's superb Software Instruments using your computer keyboard as a musical typewriter, to play the notes. Next you record a simple-voice track (your voice or a friends).

After some fun, gender-bending your voice and discovering some of the brilliant effects available in GarageBand, you learn to polish your tracks and perform some basic MIDI editing. Finally you discover the black arts of mixing: balancing the individual tracks, adding reverb and exporting the finished project to iTunes.

As you complete the projects you are given the opportunity to download my versions from www.pc-publishing.com/downloads.html, for comparison. As each consecutive project is based on the one before it, you can either continue with your own version or use mine instead; it's entirely up to you.

You may be the kind of person who likes to dip in around the middle of the book and start with a later project. No problem. It's easy enough to do because there's always a starter project available for you to download at pc-publishing.com.

At the end of each project you also have the option of completing an assignment (sometimes two or three). And if you're hungry for information, further on-topic reading follows on.

Time and tempo

In this project you will:

- Learn basics of musical time and tempo: beats and bars.
- Count and play along with GarageBand's metronome.
- Select and change a song's time signature.
- Learn the difference between 3/4 and 4/4 time signatures.
- Use the Tempo slider.

OK, here we go with your first project. Now I know you're just itching to make music of some kind. Maybe you already play a musical instrument and you're, keen to start recording straight away. Maybe you're into dance music and you've heard about how easy it is to build a tune using the brilliant pre-recorded Apple Loops supplied free with GarageBand. One thing's for sure; if you've bought this book, you're out to make music. And you can't wait to get started, right? But hold your horses, just for a few minutes. Before we actually get down to the tuneful stuff, in this project, we're going to take a quick look at two very important aspects of music making: time and tempo. A basic understanding of musical time keeping is particularly important when you work with a program like GarageBand because, unlike a conventional tape recorder, much of the time, you'll be working with a metronome.

If you're new to music making, or even if you're an amateur musician, the chances are that you won't be familiar with the concept of working to a strict metronomic beat. Believe me, it can be quite difficult, even for experienced music professionals. However, a few minutes following this simple project will show you what to expect when you hit the red button and make your first recording. And if you're an absolute beginner, you'll also learn how musical compositions are structured, how they are divided up into bars and beats and so on.

Follow these steps:

1 Create a new GarageBand project. When you start GarageBand it always opens the last song that you were working on. And as you've almost certainly been experimenting with the program before you bought this book, press Command-N, to open a new file.
2 You'll be confronted with a dialogue box asking you to name and save

Info

Invented in 1816 by Johann Maelzel, a mate of Beethoven's, a metronome is used to indicate the exact tempo of a composition. Originally a wind-up mechanical device with a swinging pendulum and a sliding weight (the slider is moved up and down the pendulum to decrease and increase the tempo), the old-fashioned metronome produced a musical tick-tock sound. By contrast, the modern metronome takes the form of a digital clock and emits a relentless bleep, usually accompanied by a flashing indicator. GarageBand's metronome is the software equivalent of this and produces a click on each beat. A setting of 60 beats per minute (bpm) means that you'll hear a beat for each second that passes because, of course, there are 60 seconds in a minute.

the song. In the shaded area of the box you'll see a tempo slider. Slide it to the left until the figure in the bpm (beats per minute) display reads 90. Leave the other parameters at their default settings for now.

3 Choose General from the GarageBand Preferences menu and set the metronome to sound during playback and recording.

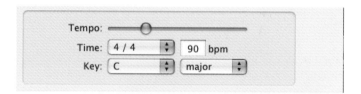

4 Now press the Play button, on the transport controls (or use your keyboard's space bar), and two things happen: the playhead begins moving to the right, along the timeline, and the metronome starts producing a steady click.

5 Press the Play button again (or use your keyboard's space bar), to pause the metronome playback for a moment.

Take a look at the timeline. You'll see that it's marked, from left to right, with a series of numbers; 1, 2, 3, 4, and so on. Each of these numbers represents the beginning of a musical measure, called a 'bar'. Notice, too, that each bar is sub-divided into four sections. Each of these sections represents a beat. What we have here, then, is a musical framework of four-beats-to-a-bar. And any music you happen to record onto this framework will be said to be in 4/4 time. The overwhelming majority of music, particularly rock, pop and jazz, has a time signature of 4/4. That's why GarageBand's opening dialogue box defaults to that setting.

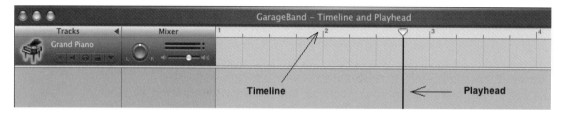

6 Press the Play button again, and this time, notice how each click of the metronome coincides with the passing of each beat, by the timeline.

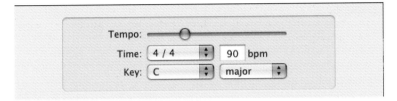

Listen closely, and you'll also notice that the first beat of each bar is signified by a different sounding click to the following three beats...

1, 2, 3, 4, | **2**, 2, 3, 4, | **3**, 2, 3, 4,

and so on.

7   Click on the song's tempo in the Time display (to the right of the transport controls – it should be displaying 90 bpm). A slider will appear. Raise the slider and the song tempo will increase. Lower the slider and the song tempo will decrease.

Of course, not all music has a time signature of 4/4. 3/4 time (three-beats-to-the-bar) is also very common. In the next step, you'll change the song's time signature to 3/4.

8   In step 1 you created a new project. New GarageBand projects always contain a single piano track by default. Click on the piano track or press Command-I on your keyboard to show the Track Info window. When it appears, click the Master Track tab. The tempo and time controls appear again.

9   From the Time drop-down menu, change the time signature to 3/4. The timeline will instantly refllect the change, clearly displaying three sub-divisions to each bar.

Press the Play button and, this time, the metronome will beat three-beats-to-the-bar...

1, 2, 3, | **2**, 2, 3, | **3**, 2, 3

and so on.

Getting to grips with rhythm, playing in time and developing the habit of counting when we play music is one of the most important, and one of the trickiest, things for beginners to learn. That's why I've devoted the very first project in this book to the subject. Take it from me - and I've taught hundreds of beginners over the years - developing the habit of counting beats and bars will pay you handsome dividends over and over again, whatever your musical aspirations. Not only will it improve your playing, it'll save you hours of wasted recording time that could be better spent writing more songs.

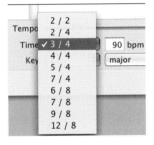

Assignments

- Experiment with the different time signatures available in GarageBand's Master Track. As you do this, note how the various time signature changes are reflected in the timeline.
- Using both 4/4 and 3/4 time signatures set the metronome to various tempos and count along with it, out loud. Note how 4/4 time has a 'square' feel as opposed to the lopsided, 'triangular' feel of 3/4 time. Note too how it's harder to accurately count slow tempos, below 90 bpm, as opposed to faster tempos, at 120 bpm and above.
- Develop your own 'mental clock'. Learn to count without a metronome. Strive for accuracy. Do this, and when you return to play along with GarageBand's metronome, you'll find it much easier to keep in time.

Start with a rhythm section

In this project you will:

- Create a virtual four piece rhythm section.
- Learn about rhythm sections and why they are important.
- Audition loops in the loop browser.
- Find, mix, and match, musically compatible Apple loops.
- Create tracks and regions.

GarageBand comes with over a thousand Apple Loops; pre-recorded, ready to play performances, pre-recorded by professional musicians. These loops are a great way to kick start a new song and particularly useful for creating rhythm tracks. As you add the loops to a composition they're automatically matched to the song's tempo and key, regardless of the pitch and tempo of the original performance. Finding suitable loops is easy too because they're organised by instrument, style and genre. You audition them first, in a loop browser, select those you like and drag and drop them onto an existing track or a blank space on the timeline. GarageBand creates a new track for each new loop you add to the timeline.

You're now going to create a four piece rhythm section, using Apple Loops. A conventional rhythm section is comprised of drums, bass, piano and guitar. It's typically used to accompany a vocal performance or a solo instrument such as a saxophone. So which instrument from the rhythm section shall we lay down first? A good many people will answer 'drums' to that question. But think about it; if the performer was rehearsing with just one of those instruments, which one is it most likely to be? Well, the answer is probably guitar or piano because they're both capable of providing a harmonic background, a chord sequence, to guide the singer or instrumentalist. We'll start with the piano.

Follow these steps:

1   Just as you did in project 1, create a new GarageBand project (press Command-N, to open a new file). Once again you'll be confronted with a dialogue box asking you to name and save the song. This time, leave the parameters in the shaded area of the box at their default settings: a tempo of 120 bpm, a time signature of 4/4 and a key signature of C.

Info

You can find loops using button view or column view in the loop browser. You switch between views by clicking the view buttons in the lower-left corner of the loop browser. The column view is fine when you know exactly the kind of instrument you want. The button view though is best when you're not quite so sure what you need. You get lots of options on display simultaneously. For example Guitars (instrument) World (genre) and Acoustic (mood) yields four Acoustic Noodling loops.

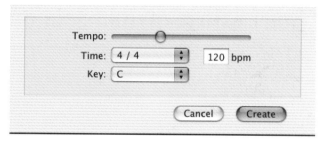

2 You set GarageBand's metronome to play during playback and recording in project 1. You did this because it was an integral part of the project. In this project you'll be working with prerecorded loops. But once the drums are playing, having the metronome clicking throughout isn't really necessary. So if it's still on, go to GarageBand's preferences menu and turn it off, by setting it to sound during recording only.

Metronome: ⊙ During recording
⃝ During playback and recording

> **Tip**
>
> You can find loops quickly using the loop browser search function. For example, to instantly locate a selection of Fusion Electric Piano loops type the words 'fusion electric piano' and press 'enter'.

3 A new song always contains a single Software Instrument track (a MIDI based track) by default, named Grand Piano. You're going to start with an electric piano instead. Press Command-L, to open the loop browser, and search for the Fusion Electric Piano 01 loop. It's in the Electric Piano section (if you select Major, in the Scale drop-down menu, the Fusion Electric Piano 01 loop appears at the top of the browser's list).

4 Drag the Fusion Electric Piano 01 loop onto the timeline – anywhere but on the existing Grand Piano track – placing it at the very beginning of bar 1. GarageBand will create a new Software Instrument track, directly beneath the Grand Piano track, entitled Electric Piano. Once on the timeline, loops become regions. You'll notice that the newly created region spans four bars (16 beats).

5 Play and cycle the region. You should now be hearing some rather delicious, spacey sounding electric piano chords.

There is a very good reason why I chose the Fusion Electric Piano loop; the playing is tasteful and uncluttered, leaving ample space, if need be, for the drums and bass to get busy. To have started with a complicated piano loop would have narrowed my options considerably. Okay, you now need some drums, to complement that rather cool piano.

> **Tip**
>
> When you're searching the loop browser and you come across a loop that you really like, add it to your favourites list (tick the Fav box, in the results list). Too view all your favourites in the results list, click the Favorites keyword button in button view. Alternatively, select the Favourites keyword type in column view.

6 Select the All Drums category in the loop browser (select Any, in the Scale drop-down menu). The browser will now display hundreds of drum loops.

7 Begin playing and cycling the electric piano loop again and, at the same time, start auditioning drummers! That's right, you can audition the loops by simply clicking on them whilst GarageBand is playing a song. I've chosen the Live Edgy Drums 05 loop, so for now, select that one.

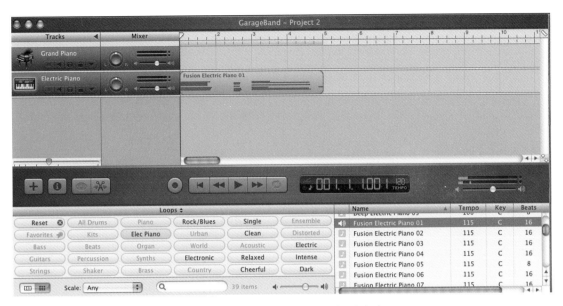

8 Drag the Live Edgy Drums 05 loop onto the timeline, immediately below the electric piano region. GarageBand will create a Real Instrument track (an audio track) named Drum Kit and convert the loop into a region.

9 Press C, to cycle the regions. Alternatively press the cycle button, on the Transport controls. Together, the electric piano and drums create a nice groove. Things sound good already.

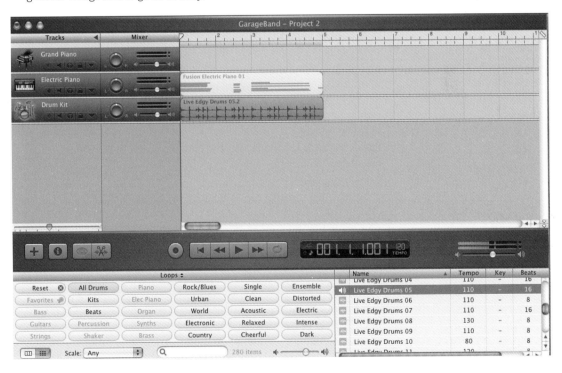

Choosing a drum loop to complement the electric piano was easy enough. After all, there are hundreds to choose from and they all adjust to GarageBand's song tempo. I chose the Edgy Drum type for its sense of urgency, which makes a nice contrast to the super relaxed, cool sounding electric piano loop. Selecting a bass loop requires more thought. There are several things to consider. Do you need an electric or an acoustic bass? Or maybe a bass synthesiser? Which do you need; a relaxed or intense playing style?

10 Select the Bass category in the loop browser. (select Any, in the Scale drop-down menu). Over a hundred bass loops will appear in the browser; far too many to trawl through, one at a time. You're now going to filter some of them out. You're building a conventional rhythm section, right? In that case, you don't need the bass synths. That leaves you with a choice of either electric or acoustic bass. Both types will work so which instrument you choose is largely a matter of personal taste. For the sake of expediency, why not choose an acoustic upright bass?

11 Select the Acoustic category (keep the Bass category selected too). The number of available loops will considerably diminish, making it far easier to find a loop that fits the bill. Now what about style? Well, so far, despite the drum loop, things sound pretty relaxed, so:

12 Add 'Relaxed' to the Bass and Acoustic categories, to narrow things down a bit more.

13 Cycle the song and audition a few loops. You'll find that some will fit better than others. In some cases the playing will sound far too busy; in other words, they contain too many notes. In other cases, some of the notes played in a loop will clash with those of the piano. At this point, I think it's better to reduce the number of choices even further.

14 The electric piano loop is in a major key. Select Major, in the Scale drop-down menu. The browser will now display just ten loops. Now you needn't necessarily have gone quite as far as that to get a loop that fits, but doing so has demonstrated how you can use the GargeBand loop search effectively.

15 Select the Woody Latin Bass 04 loop and drag it onto the timeline. GarageBand will create a third track called Acoustic Bass and convert the loop into a region.

It's time to add a fourth instrument to your standard rhythm section. This will typically be either an electric or acoustic guitar. Unfortunately, straightforward strummed guitar loops are thin on the ground in GarageBand's selection of Apple Loops. However, there are lots of picked lines to choose from.

16 Select the Classic Rock Steel 01 loop, which can be found by jointly selecting the Guitars and Acoustic categories in the loop browser. Drag the loop onto the timeline. A fourth track, entitled Acoustic Guitar will be created, along with another 16 beat region.

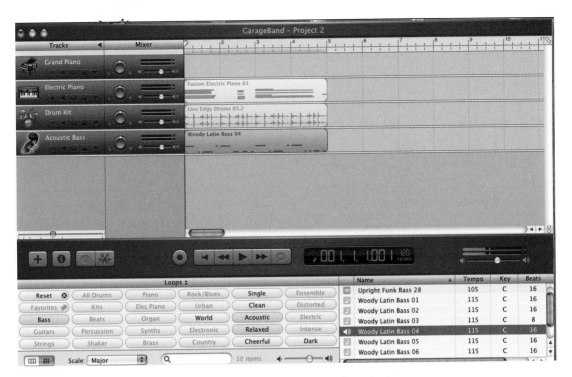

I chose that particular guitar lick because of its simplicity. It's unobtrusive but still manages to cut through and compliment the electric piano. Neither will it interfere with any vocal or instrumental line that might be added later.

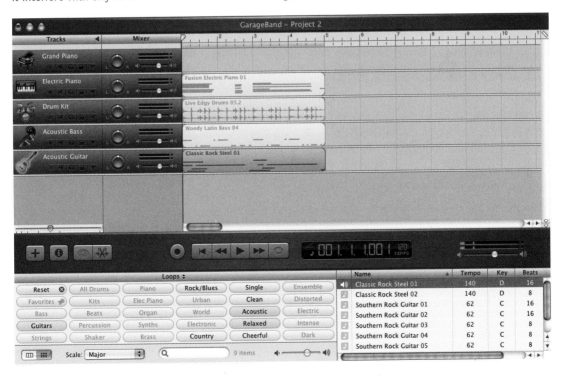

17 Save this project and name it (project 2) because you will be using it again, as a basis for project 3. You can download my version, for comparison, at http://www.pc-publishing.com/downloads.html.

Assignments

- Experiment with the above project by substituting my choice of loops with those of your own. Do this one loop at a time and, as you do so, consider carefully the following points:

  (a) When substituting a piano, guitar or bass loop; listen carefully, to make sure the actual notes played fit with the other instruments. Even if your knowledge of musical theory is limited, you'll know, instinctively, if something sounds wrong. So hunt around until you find a loop that sounds correct. But don't worry about mixing keys. If the notes in one loop are clashing with the notes of another, it's due to the actual harmonic structure of the music and has nothing to do with either loop's original key. GarageBand always transposes any loop you choose to fit the song's key.

  (b) Generally speaking, for conventional styles of music, matching loops will be easier if you keep them to similar tempo ranges. For example, a drum loop recorded at 125 bpm is more likely to sit well with a bass loop recorded at 140 bpm than another, recorded at 75 bpm. However, this is not a hard and fast rule. Sometimes, mixing and matching widely varying tempos can yield surprisingly good results. So experiment and use your own judgement.

- From scratch, build three conventional rhythm sections of your own. Give each one a different instrumentation and musical style. Keep them short, with single regions (or groups of regions) that span four bars (16 beats). Also select different tempos for each assignment; for example 80, 110 and 140 bpm.

More about rhythm sections

At the heart of any good band lies the rhythm section. These are the instruments crucial to any style of modern danceable music.

A traditional rhythm section is comprised of drums, bass, guitar and piano, a direct descendant of the big bands, popular in the 1930s and 1940s. In those days, their main function was to drive the music along, providing the 'engine room' for the lead players, the brass and saxophones.

Today, entire rock bands are comprised of just the instruments of the rhythm section. Their main purpose now, of course, is to provide a backing for the lead singer. Electronic dance tracks, too, feature elements from a traditional rhythm section, drum and bass loops being the most obvious example. Let's take a look at the individual instruments in a typical rhythm section and briefly examine their role within it.

Drums

The drum kit is the most crucial instrument in the rhythm section. Now a drum kit can be big or small but ask a drummer which parts of his kit he just couldn't do without and he'll answer: the bass drum (often referred to, these days, as the kick drum), the snare drum and the high-hat cymbals. These are the three main elements needed to drive the music along. Other parts of the drummer's arsenal such as toms and cymbals, although important, are used mainly for embellishment.

Locate the loop named Straight Up Beat 01, drag it onto the timeline and examine it. This is the archetypal rock drum pattern, used countless times over the last fifty years or so.

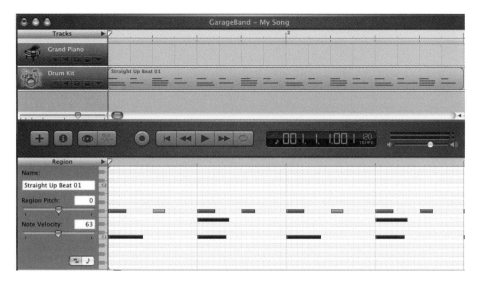

The bass drum (C1) provides a relentless four-to-the-bar, a solid foundation, at the bottom end. The snare (E1) breaks the monotony, on the second and third beats of the bar. A closed hi-hat (F#1) breaks the beat down further, into 1/8 notes.

Bass

In the early days of popular music and jazz, the bass line was always played on an upright, wooden bass. It's still used today, of course, and you'll find quite a few upright bass loops in GarageBand. The Cool, Walking and Funk Upright Basses and the Woody Latin Bass sets are good examples. But most groups, especially, rock bands, use electric guitars. Electronic dance music is more inclined to favour bass loops played on a synthesiser such as GarageBand's Techno Bass collection.

In a conventional rhythm section, the bass player works closely with the drummer, often playing notes that match the bass drum, further helping to propel the music and strengthen the bottom end. Of course, that's not always the case and a good bass player also knows how to break away from the bass drum, embellishing the underlying rhythmic structure without losing the pulse.

Guitar

In the days of the big bands, rhythm guitarists usually played chords in a straight four-to-the-bar fashion. Being uncluttered, it worked very well against the complexity of the main brass and saxophone lines. Anything more would have been over complicated and unnecessary. However, the modern day rhythm guitarist usually finds himself in a small group environment and has far more freedom. Naturally, what he plays depends very much on the style of the music but often the rhythm guitar part is influenced by the hi-hat pattern. The rhythm guitar part is usually made up of chords, such as GarageBand's Strummed Acoustic loops, but not always. Sometimes single note lines, of a rhythmic nature, like GarageBand's Funky Electric set, do the job just as well.

Piano

In today's rhythm sections, electric pianos are far more common than their acoustic counterparts, for the simple reasons of economics and portability. Like the guitar, in the days of the big band, the pianist kept things simple with four-to-the-bar style chords, occasionally filling in the gaps between the horns. In modern popular music the pianist has far more freedom. However, if a guitarist is also present, the main concern is to avoid getting in each other's way. Common sense usually prevails with the piano playing elaborate rhythmic patterns against simple guitar chords and vice versa.

Examples of straight four-to-the-bar piano chords can be found in the 70s Ballad Piano set. You'll find a more elaborate version of this technique in the Southern Rock Piano collection. Under Electric Piano, check out the spacey chords of the Fusion Electric Piano set (plenty of room for busy guitar loops alongside these) and, by way of contrast, Upbeat Electric Piano 03.

GarageBand as a loop production tool

When sequencers first appeared, musicians were presented with a wealth of production techniques, previously impossible with just a tape recorder. One of the most obvious was the facility to record a section of music into a MIDI track and loop it repeatedly, for as long as necessary. In the right hands, this technique can be used to compose and produce exciting, rhythmically driven, electronic dance music. It takes many forms with 'techno' and 'house' perhaps being the best known.

Once sequencers were capable of recording audio as well as MIDI data, it wasn't long before dance music producers were importing pre-recorded audio files and looping them alongside their MIDI tracks. But of course, unless the imported audio files had been recorded at an identical speed to that of the song they were working on, the two types of track data would be out of sync. The obvious answer was to time stretch (or shrink) and pitch shift the audio files. It could be done in a conventional sequencer but the process was far from easy.

So, in response to the growing popularity of loop based music production, a few years ago several 'audio only' sequencers appeared on the market. Products such as Ableton Live provided instant time stretching facilities for mixing and matching audio samples regardless of their individual pitch and tempo. Several other audio sequencers such as Fruity Loops and Cool Edit Pro did much the same thing. These easy-to-use sequencers were, and still are, extremely popular and attracted a whole new generation to computer music making. But until recently these programs lacked MIDI functionality and couldn't run MIDI tracks alongside the audio loops. Now, most of them do – and so does GarageBand.

Changing instruments and sounds

In this project you will:

- Learn about the Track Info window.
- Change an instrument's sounds, on a specific track.
- Learn about Software Instruments and their associated tracks.
- Learn about Real Instruments and their associated tracks.

In project 2, you created a short piece of music using Apple loops. The chosen instruments were those used in a typical rhythm section. But do you know that you can alter the sound output of these loops? Software Instrument loops, on MIDI based tracks, can be set to playback entirely different instruments. Real Instrument loops, on audio tracks, can be treated with a wide range of effects that are capable of radically altering their sound. It's time to experiment.

Follow these steps:

1   Open your finished version of Project 2. Alternatively, download my version at http://www.pc-publishing.com/downloads.html. You don't really need that empty Grand Piano track; so delete it (Track > Delete Track). Save a new version, this time, as Project 3.

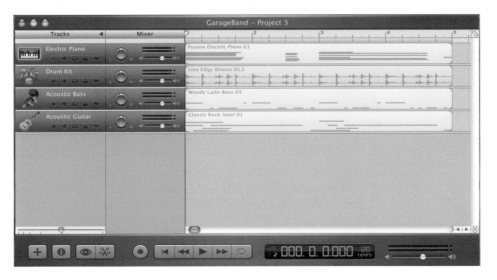

Tip

Use your computer's keyboard spacebar to start and stop GarageBand. If the track info window is open, it will continue to float.

2 Select the electric piano track and press Command-I. This opens the Track Info window. You'll see that it's labelled a Software Instrument. The track info window is divided into two sections. Instrument categories are listed on the left. The individual instruments themselves are listed on the right.

3 Select the instrument called Grand Piano Punchy from the Pianos and Keyboards instrument category (you'll be asked by GarageBand to name and save your current settings – save them as Fusion Electric Piano 01).

Note that because you saved it, the Fusion Electric Piano has been added to the instrument list. GarageBand has also renamed the track as Grand Piano Punchy.

4 Play the sequence, to hear the difference. While the song is playing, try out a few more pianos (you don't necessarily have to stop GarageBand each time). Each one will change the character of the song in some way.

Tip

To listen to a track by itself, click on its Solo button (the headphone icon in the track's header).

So how come the original electric piano region can play all these different pianos? This is because a Software Instrument track is really a MIDI track in GarageBand. The recorded notes (captured as MIDI data) are playing back a GarageBand Software Instrument. And you're not just restricted to pianos either; you can playback any kind of software instrument. Try this:

5 Select the instrument category named Strings and choose Hollywood Strings from the individual instrument list. Now play the song. What a difference!

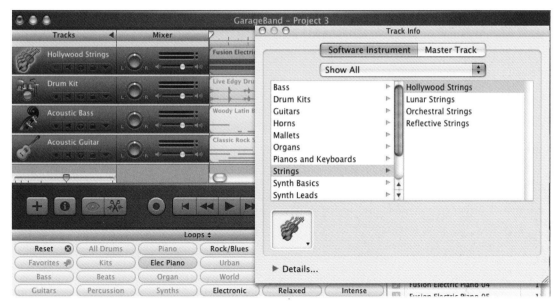

6 To get back to our original electric piano settings, select Fusion Electric
   Piano 01 in the track info window (you saved it earlier).
7 Now select the Drum Kit track and open the track info window. You'll
   notice that, this time, it's a Real Instrument track. What you heard here
   was an audio recording of a musician playing a real drum kit. The window
   is divided into two halves. On the left is a list of instrument categories.
   On the right is a list of individual instruments. Near the bottom are
   channel input settings, which for the moment you can ignore.
8 Select Crunchy Drums from the individual instrument list and play the
   track (you'll be asked by GarageBand to name and save your current
   settings – save them as Live Edgy Drums). Wow! That's a pretty messed

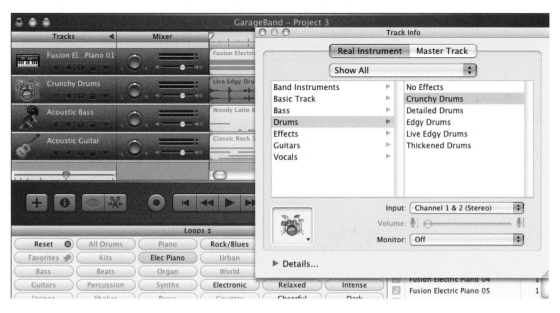

up drum sound and fully lives up to its name. What you're hearing now, of course, is not really another instrument but the same audio recording (the Live Edgy Drum loop) being treated with a distortion effect. You'll be taking a closer look at effects later on. For now, just have fun experimenting with the different pre-sets on the list.

9 When you've finished trying out the various effects return the track to its original setting of Live Edgy Drums (if you saved it, it will be on the list).

10 Save this project and name it (project 3) because we shall be using it again, as a basis for project 4. You can download my version, for comparison, at http://www.pc-publishing.com/downloads.html.

Assignments

- Using the track info box, experiment with different instrument sounds, to alter the character of project 3. For example, substituting an organ for the acoustic guitar will send the tune in a different direction; same notes played on a completely different sounding instrument.
- Using the track info box, experiment with different effects on the project 3 drum track. For example, selecting Vocal > Live Performance, adds a sense of acoustic space to the drums.

GarageBand as an audio recorder

Before programs like GarageBand existed the recording industry used multi-track reel-to-reel tape recorders to record live music. The sound waves produced by musical instruments and singers were captured with microphones, converted to electrical signals and stored on magnetic tape. Different instruments were assigned to different tracks. When the recording was complete it was mixed down to 2-track stereo tape.

Recording with GarageBand is a similar process to old fashioned tape recording but instead of the sound waves being captured on magnetic tape, they're sampled and stored as digital code on your Mac's hard drive; the data is subsequently displayed as a sound wave on an audio track. However, Apple, in their wisdom, decided to rename their audio tracks as Real Instrument tracks; a confusing description, to say the least, because any sound can be recorded on an audio track including the human voice.

GarageBand as a sequencer

Today's top recording software began life in the 1980s, as MIDI only applications. At that time the average computer didn't possess the necessary processing power required to handle audio recording. However, they could manage MIDI data and because musicians and recording engineers were already using them, the software developers modelled their sequencing programs on multitrack tape recorders. But instead of audio tracks they had MIDI tracks.

The familiar tape recorder style interface proved popular and MIDI sequencing took off in a big way. For the first time, musicians could record their synthesiser performances as data (not audio) onto MIDI tracks. On playback, the sequencer transmitted the recorded information back to the instrument it was originally played on. In other words, the computer was now controlling the synthesiser. If a wrong note had been played the musician simply corrected it, by editing the data on the MIDI track. Recording it again for the sake of a single mistake was no longer necessary.

By the mid 90s computers were much more powerful and sequencing software programs were running audio and MIDI tracks simultaneously. It was around this time that software instruments first appeared. This was another giant leap forwards because musicians could now record onto MIDI tracks and control software synthesisers as an alternative to routing the data back to their hardware instruments. These days the major sequencers such as Logic and Cubase include a comprehensive set of software instruments with their applications which can be used as plug-ins. And so, too, does GarageBand.

It may be an entry level program but as a sequencer GarageBand operates just like the big boys and includes a abundant collection of software instruments – basses, guitars, synths and so on – that can be controlled from a MIDI track.

But Apple decided to confuse everybody again by renaming GarageBand's MIDI tracks as Software Instrument tracks. Of course, they're really just the same as other sequencer MIDI tracks; you can use them to record your performance using a MIDI keyboard and edit the data afterwards.

However, unlike most sequencing software, GarageBand cannot relay the recorded data to any external hardware synthesisers that you might own. To do that, you'll need to upgrade to a sequencer like Logic or Cubase. Editing MIDI data on a Software Instrument track (MIDI track) is also restricted but for general song writing and entry level sequencing there are just enough features to produce the goods.

Extending your tune

In this project you will:

- Use repetition as a musical arranging device (without boring your listeners).
- Loop regions.
- Move regions.
- Choose a value for the timeline grid.
- Use snap-to-grid when working with regions.
- Use the zoom slider.
- Toggle the time display between bars-and-beats and absolute time (hrs. min. sec.).

Basically, what you've done so far, in projects 2 and 3, is discover how GarageBand works as a loop production tool. But of course, four bars of music is ludicrously short and, at this tempo, lasts for only six seconds. Fortunately loop based music is repetitive by nature and extending this composition is a simple matter of looping and moving regions.

- To loop a region: grab its upper right-hand corner (the cursor becomes a loop pointer).

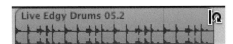

Now drag to the right and extend the loop as far as necessary.

- To move a region: grab it in the centre or anywhere but the edges and drag it to a new position.

Follow these steps:

1 Open your version of Project 3. Alternatively, download my version from http://www.pc-publishing.com/downloads.html. Save a new version and name it Project 4.

Of course, just looping all four tracks will result in boring, monotonous music (a trap that's easily fallen into) so how can you make it interesting? Well, at the moment, all four tracks are playing together so why not create some spaces?

Before you move anything, click on the small ruler icon (top right corner) and make sure the snap-to-grid setting is set to a 1/4 note. Doing so will ensure all your looping and moving will snap to single beats.

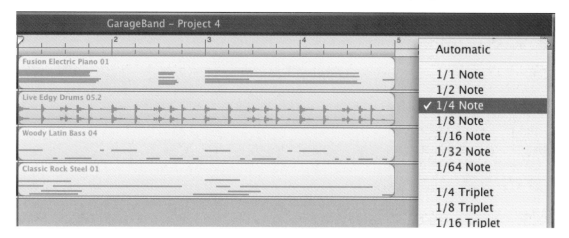

You're going to use one of the simplest, and still most effective arranging techniques in the book; have each instrument of the rhythm section enter the picture one at a time. Count Basie used it on his big band classic, "One O'Clock Jump". Countless soul bands have used it over the years, to introduce members of the band on stage. And the same technique is commonly heard on modern day dance music tracks. So, if it's good enough for them, it's good enough for us. But who's going to start? The answer, of course, is the drummer.

2 Loop the Live Edgy Drum region, so that it ends at bar 21. Doing this gives us plenty of space to allow the other instruments to gradually enter the fray.

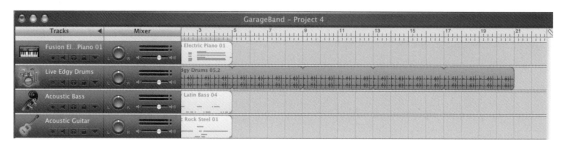

3 Move the Fusion Electric Piano region so that it starts at the beginning of bar 13 and then loop it so that it ends, like the drum loop, at bar 21.
4 Move the Woody Latin Bass region so that it starts at the beginning of bar 5 and then loop it, so that it ends at bar 21.
5 Last but not least, move the Classic Rock Steel region so that it starts at bar 9 and then loop it, so that it ends, like the others, at bar 21.

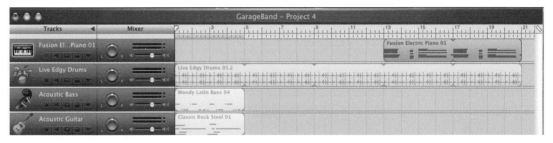

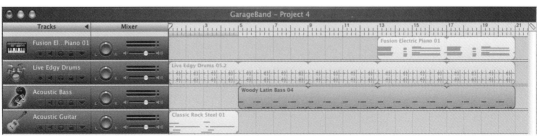

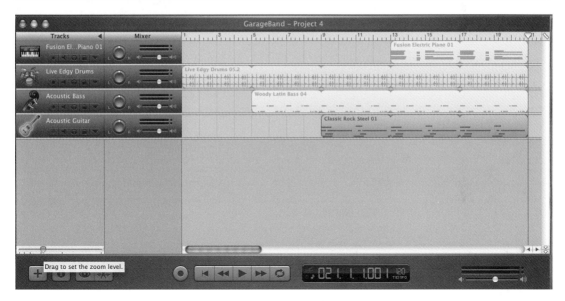

6 Turn off the Cycle button and play the new, extended version through.

Okay, that's not exactly a revolutionary arranging technique but it has extended the piece to 40 seconds without endlessly repeating the same four bars and without adding any new loops.

The drums play alone for four bars. Of course, you could have them play for longer, but that would be boring, unless you varied the beat pattern or added a new loop.

The bass enters at bar 5. Why choose the bass, and not the guitar or piano? Well, it's the natural choice; it sounds fuller and provides that all important bottom end. Things will sound slightly empty if you choose guitar or piano to play at this point. Again, without variation, four bars with the drums and bass playing together is long enough.

Tip

To view the entire 20 bars at once; move the zoom slider (bottom left corner) to the left.

Either of the two remaining instruments, guitar or piano, can enter next. After trying them both, I settled on the guitar because this loop contains just single, picked notes (no strumming) and they set up an air of expectancy. Once again, four bars are enough.

The sense of expectation provided by the guitar is fulfilled, when at bar 13, the electric piano plays eight bars of block chords.

As I mentioned earlier, the piece is now 40 seconds long. And how do I know that? Take a look at the time display on the transport controls. The display is most likely set to bars-and-beats and as you would expect, shows a reading of 21 bars.

7   Click on the tiny note icon, to change the reading to absolute time (hrs. min. sec.). It will now read as 40 seconds.
8   Click on the tiny clock icon, to change the display back to bars and beats.

Note and Clock icons

Save this project and name it (project 4) because you will be using it again as a basis for project 5. You can download my version, for comparison, at http://www.pc-publishing.com/downloads.html.

Assignment

Using project 2 as a starting point, invent your own arrangement by repeating and moving loops on the timeline. This time though, have the drums enter last.

Repetition and variation

Memorable tunes rely heavily on repetition. How else can people remember them? They expect repetition. It's a subconscious human desire. Expectancy, and the fulfilment of it, plays a vital role in the memorability stakes. Your listeners will rapidly lose interest in your tunes if you don't repeat anything. The danger here, of course, is predictability, especially if you're relying heavily on loops. To alleviate boredom in a repeated section composers use a technique known as repetition and variation.

So far you've only used a handful of loops and frankly, there's not much scope for variation, other than reordering them or leaving some out, to create gaps. Even so, whatever you're writing, if you want it to sound interesting, remember that repetition and variation go hand in hand. It's a balancing act; too much of either will bore people senseless.

Adding a horn section

In this project you will:

- Construct a horn line, using a selection of different loops.
- Filter for more relevant results in the loop browser, by limiting your search to loops that are close to the song key.
- Hide notes in a loop, by resizing the region that contains them.
- Edit the musical content of loops and regions, both on the timeline and in the track editor.
- Split regions.
- Alter the timeline's snap value.

So far, you have sequenced 20 bars of music, which lasts for 40 seconds. That's not very long, is it? However to repeat it all again, without any variation, runs the risk of boring your listeners. Getting inside those loops and editing them will be covered later in this book. So for the time being, introducing a new element to the music is the best way forward. What's needed

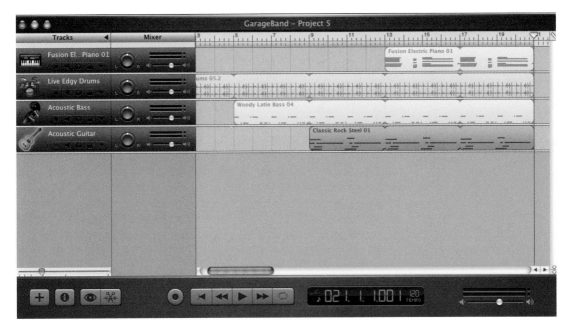

is some melodic content, a lead line of some kind. Ladies and Gents; meet the horn section.

Follow these steps:

1   Open your version of Project 4 (or download my version from http://www.pc-publishing.com/downloads.html). Save a new version and name it Project 5.

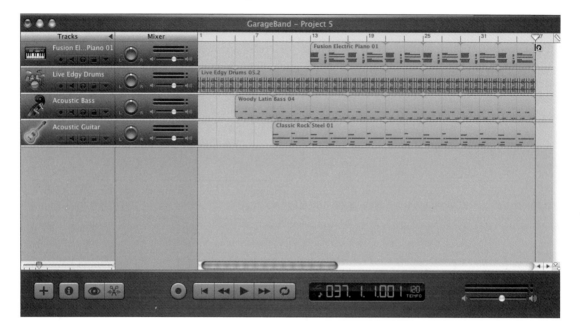

2   Loop all four regions so that they end at bar 37.

Finding suitable horn section loops in GarageBand isn't as easy as finding rhythm section loops. For a start, there are fewer of them and they aren't categorized in the loop browser button view.

3   Using column view in the loop browser, select Instruments > Horn > Horn. Find the R&B Horn Section loops; there are 13 in the series.

Now, your tune is in the key of C and several of these horn section loops were recorded in distant keys. And because they're all Real Instrument loops, once transposed, they may sound odd. They'll sound in tune, of course, because GarageBand will transpose them into the key of C. But pitch-shifted trumpets, particularly when playing high notes, sound squeaky when transposed upwards. And the lower notes, when transposed downwards, tend to sound muddy. So you need to choose loops that are either in the same key as your tune – the key of C – or pretty close to it.

4   Open the GarageBand preferences and ensure that 'Filter for more relevant results' is checked in the Keyword Browser section. This will limit the loop browser search to loops that are within two semitones of the song key.

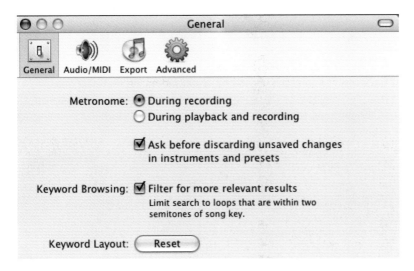

OK, you should now be left with just three R&B Horn Section loops, No. 5 and 9, in the key of C and No. 8, in the key of D. Not many to work with, is it? Never-mind, even with such limited material as this, with a little ingenuity we should be able to put together some decent horn lines. I'm a great believer in the concept of 'less is more'.

5   Select the R&B Horn Section loop and drag it onto the timeline at bar 21. GarageBand will create a real instrument track, called Horn | Wind, and convert the loop into a new region, spanning four bars (16 beats).

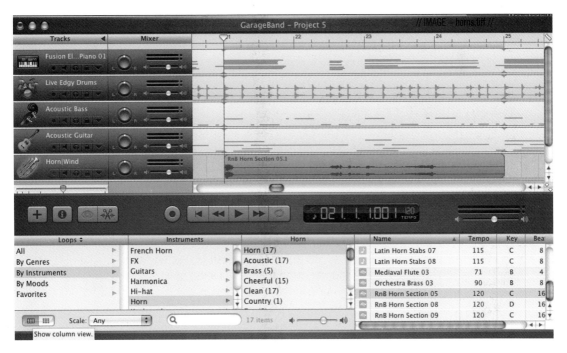

6 Set up a cycle (bars 21 – 25) and play it through a few times. It's a great horn line and kicks off beautifully with a powerful 'stab' but the last note isn't fitting too well with the track. It's not exactly clashing but what a pity they didn't play something else at that point, something more rhythmic. However, you can easily fix this by simply hiding the offending note.

7 Resize the region, by dragging the right edge backwards, so that it ends at the beginning of bar 23. This will effectively cut out the last note played.

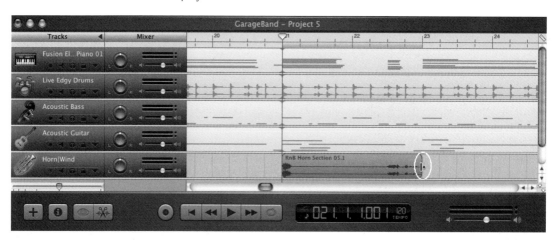

8 Set up a cycle (bars 21 – 23) and play it round again. It sounds a whole lot better, that's for sure. You could just leave it at that but the phrase sounds incomplete; something more is needed.

9 Drag the loop named R&B Horn Section 08 onto the horn track at the beginning of bar 23. A four bar region (16 beats) will be created.

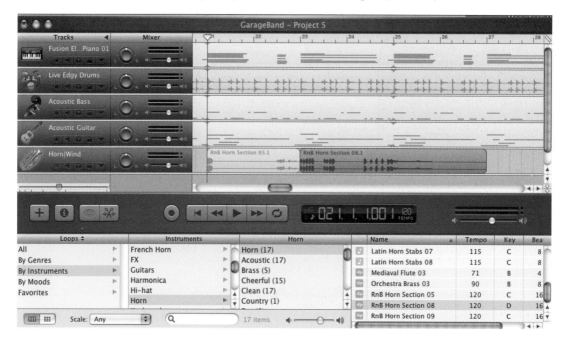

10 Turn off the cycle button and play the song from bar 23. That's much better. The two loops (regions) fit well together. Trouble is, the notes from bar 24 onwards don't fit the song. No problem; we'll simply cover them up, as we did with the first horn loop.

11 Drag the right edge of R&B Horn Section 08 back to the beginning of bar 24.

12 Set up a four bar cycle, between bars 21 and 25 and play the song. Great! We now have a punchy horn line that perfectly complements the song.

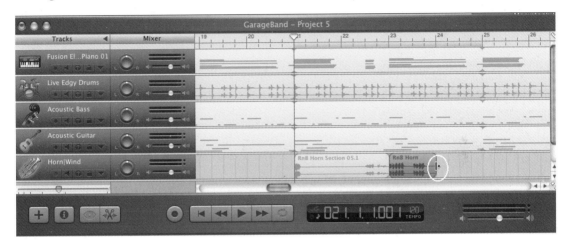

13 Select both horn regions and drag copies to bar 25. That'll give you eight bars of horns (bars 21 – 29).

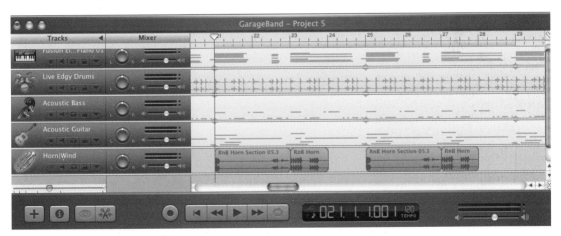

It would be nice to keep those horns going for a while longer but to repeat them again without variation would be boring. So once again you need new material.

14 Find the loop named R&B Horn Section 09 and drag it onto the horn track, at bar 29.

15 Set up a cycle between bars 29 and 33 and play the song. This loop also fits well but, personally, I don't care for the first notes of each phrase. Hide them:

16 Double click the R&B Horn Section 09 region, to open the track editor. The Real Instrument editor is revealed and displays the waveforms of the recorded audio. Because the horns played spiky, clearly defined notes, you'll notice that each note played has a corresponding audio waveform. You're going to hide the very first one. You could do it on the timeline but it's much easier to do it here, in the instrument editor.

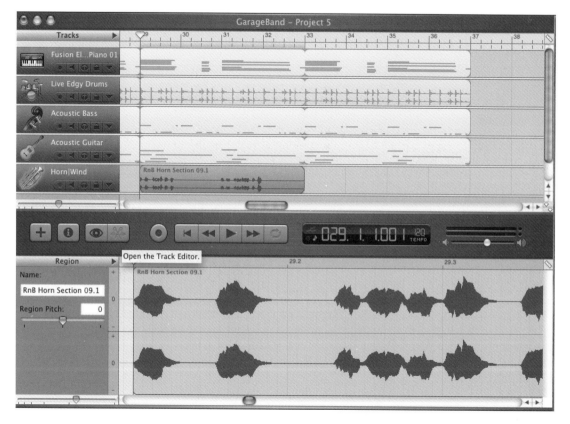

17 In the Real Instrument editor, grab the bottom left corner of the region and drag it to the right, until you've completely covered the first waveform. Notice that your actions are reflected in the timeline.

18 Play the song now and the first note of the region will not be heard (see pic top of opposite page).

The very same note offends my ear again, at bar 31. The simplest method of dealing with this is to split the region and, as before, hide the offending note.

19 Select the region and with the playhead at bar 32, press Command-T. The region will be split into two separate regions named R&B Horn Section 09.2 and 09.3 respectively.

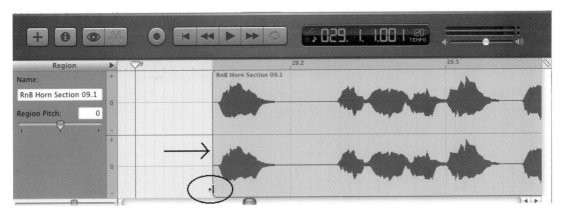

20 As you did before, in the Real Instrument editor, grab the bottom left corner of the region named R&B Horn Section 09.3 and drag it to the right, until you've completely covered the first waveform.

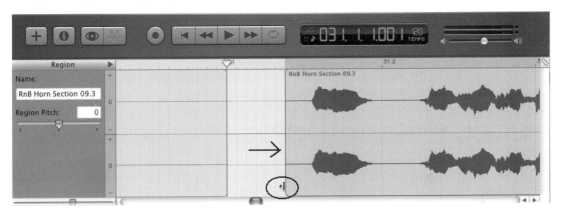

21 Cycle the song again (bars 29 – 33) to hear the difference. Losing the first note of each phrase means the horns now enter on an offbeat; they skip along more.

22 To finish up, select the two horn regions between bars 29 and 33 and copy them to bar 33. Of course, play them now and they'll enter a half beat too soon. And if you try moving them by half a beat, they'll just skip to the second beat instead, not what we want at all. So what's the reason for their stubborn behaviour? It's because the snap value for the timeline grid is set to 1/4 Note. It needs to be changed to a 1/8 Note value.

23 Click on the tiny ruler (top right corner) and choose 1/8 Note, from the drop down menu.

24 Now move the newly created regions, at bar 33, a half beat (1/8 note) to the right. Now they'll sound correct.

That's it. You've created a snappy horn arrangement from just three short loops. If you use the Zoom slider, to create an overview of the entire 36 bars, your song should look something like the screenshot below.

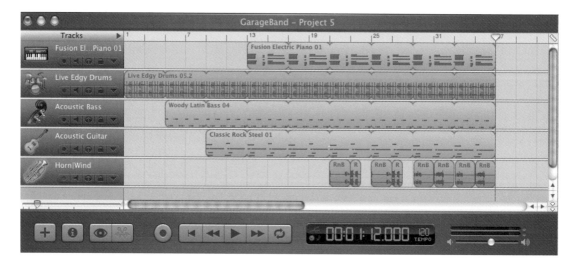

25 Save this project and name it (project 5) because you will be using it again as a basis for project 6. You can download my version, for comparison, at http://www.pc-publishing.com/downloads.html.

Assignment

In the project above, you introduced melodic content to your tune, using a horn section. Using the same techniques, add melodic content of your own. Follow these guidelines:

* Look for melodic lines and riffs that complement your rhythm section. Suggested categories: organs, synths and saxophones.
* If necessary, turn on the keyword-browsing filter in the GarageBand preferences, to narrow the search to loops played in a nearby key.
* Mute the recently constructed horn track, to avoid confusion.

More about horn sections

In a symphony orchestra the horn section is comprised of instruments known as French horns. But pop, rock and R&B horn sections don't usually contain these instruments at all. The term 'horns' is used loosely to describe various combinations of trumpets, saxophones and trombones. A typical rock horn section uses trumpet (sometimes two), tenor sax and trombone.

Although harmonies are commonly used when writing for horns, unison sounds produce a very powerful effect. The horns in your project are playing in unison.

Info

In musical terms the word 'unison' means that more than one instrument is playing the same note(s). This provides a fuller, more powerful sound than if those instruments were playing in harmony (although not necessarily a richer texture).

Playing and recording a software instrument

In this project you will:

- Learn about the GarageBand keyboard.
- Use the GarageBand Musical Typing keyboard.
- Play a scale of C major.
- Create a new Software Instrument track.
- Record onto a Software Instrument track.
- Add a string section to your tune.
- Learn about latency.
- Use GarageBand's Fix Timing feature, to correct any errors in your playing.
- Draw, shorten and lengthen notes in the track editor.

So far, in this book, you've only used GarageBand as a loop based production tool, using other people's pre-recorded music. But it's time to move on and record some music of your own. You can record onto both Real Instrument tracks and Software Instrument tracks but the two methods are distinctly different. Let's deal with the software instruments first.

Follow these steps:

1 Open your finished version of Project 5. Alternatively, download my version at http://www.pc-publishing.com/downloads.html. Save a new version and name it Project 6.
2 Select the Fusion Electric Piano track and press Command-K, to open the keyboard.

This is the original GarageBand keyboard, the most basic method of playing a software instrument (see pic overleaf). But it's really only good for auditioning the various sounds on offer. Playing a piano style keyboard with a mouse just isn't practical. To play anything half decent you'll need a proper MIDI keyboard and a MIDI interface of some kind. However, if you don't yet have a MIDI set-up of your own, you can, for now, use GarageBand's on-screen keyboard instead. It's fine for gaining a basic understanding of how GarageBand's software instruments work.

3 With your mouse, press down a note on the keyboard. You should hear the Fusion Electric Piano sound. Note that you can only play one note at a time

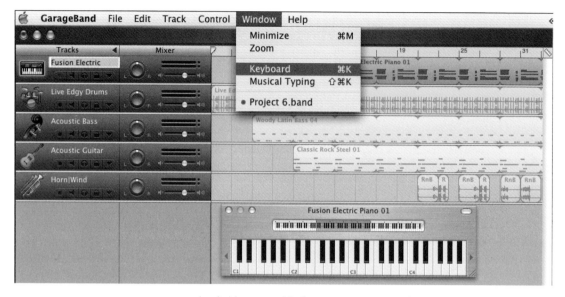

and switching smoothly from one note to another, other than adjacent ones, is difficult, to say the least. Another, better method of playing the Fusion Electric Piano is to use GarageBand's Musical Typing feature.

4   Keep the Fusion Electric Piano track selected and this time, press Shift-Command-K. A hybrid keyboard appears; combining the keys of both a computer keyboard and a piano keyboard.

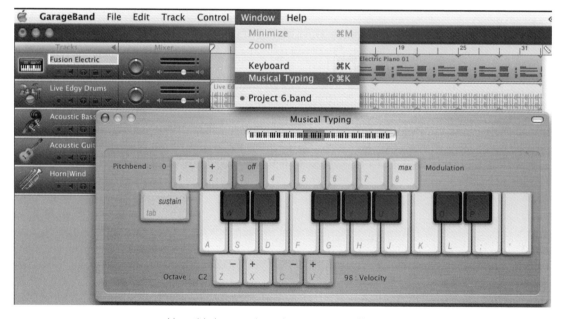

Now this is very clever because, even if you don't own a MIDI keyboard, you can actually play a simple musical line and record it. The keys of a piano keyboard have been mapped to those of a standard computer keyboard. If you've ever played piano, you'll recognise the layout. Okay, it's time for your piano lesson.

5   Before you play anything, move either up or down through the available octaves by pressing the yellow keys; Z (down) or X (up). Set the Octave display to C3.

6   The Velocity display should read 98 (which is fine). If it doesn't adjust it something similar using the orange keys; C and V.

7   From left to right, play each white key, in turn (A to K on your computer keyboard). That was a scale of C major. But you can also play chords.

8   Press down A, D and G, simultaneously. That's a chord of C major.

9   Now cursor down to the Acoustic Bass track. Set the Octave display to C2.

10 Try playing this commonly used bass line: (left to right) A, D, G, H, U, (and back again) H, G, D.

Okay, now that you've got the hang of it you're going to add a simple string line to the song.

11 Open GarageBand's preferences and ensure that the metronome is set to click only during recording, not during playback.

12 In the Control menu, activate Count In. While you're there, tick Metronome and Snap to Grid as well.

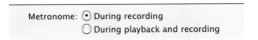

13 Select a 1/4 Note value for the timeline grid (click on the tiny ruler, top right corner).

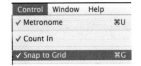

You're going to create a new Software Instrument track.

14 Press Alt-Command-N, to create a new track. Alternatively use Track > New Track. Choose the Software Instrument category and select Strings > Hollywood Strings.

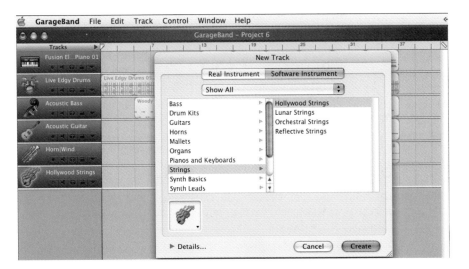

You're now going to record on the new track, so make sure it's selected.

15 Place the Playhead at bar 1.
16 Open Musical Typing (Shift-Command-K).
17 Change the Octave display back to C3.

Now, you're probably wondering what on earth I'm going to ask you to record. Don't worry. All you have to do is press down K, on your computer keyboard. This will play the musical note C. Try it now.

18 On your computer keyboard, press down K and hold. You'll hear the note C, played by the Hollywood Strings. You can also use your mouse to play the note, in the Musical Typing on-screen window.

Just one more thing, before you start recording. After you press the record button, you'll hear four clicks of the metronome, before the drums join in. Wait until the playhead reaches bar 9, before you play anything. If you can, count those eight bars through (for help on this, see Project 1), like this:

1, 2, 3, 4 | **2**, 2, 3, 4 | **3**, 2, 3, 4 | **4**, 2, 3, 4

and so on. Right then, off you go.

19 Press the Record button; the metronome clicks for one bar (four beats) and the playhead begins it's travels, to the right. When it reaches bar 8:
20 Press K, on your computer keyboard, and hold it down until you hear the horns enter, at bar 21. As soon as they enter, release K and press your computer's spacebar, to stop the song.
21 Place the Playhead a few beats before bar 9 and playback the music you've just recorded.
22 Open the Track Editor and enable the graphic view. Your newly recorded string line should look something like the pic at the top of the opposite page.

The green line, in the editor, represents the note you played whilst holding down K, on your computer keyboard. Look closely and you'll see that it corresponds to the note C4, on the vertically displayed piano keyboard (on the left).

In the screen shot at the top of the opposite page, I played the note, in time, bang on the first beat of bar 9. This isn't easy, particularly if you're a beginner. Also, depending upon your computer's specifications, the Musical Typing feature may suffer from latency, and your playing, no matter how accurate, will probably be delayed a little.

So, if your string line looks like the one in the second screen shot, and starts a little late, fear not, because you can fix it easily enough.

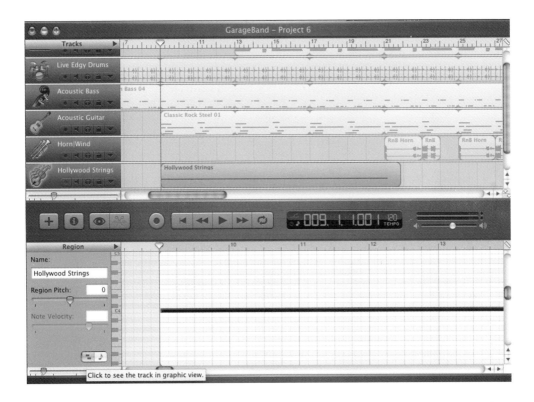

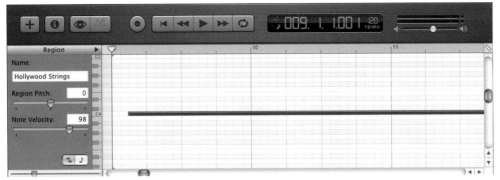

23 If your note was recorded late, simply drag it to the left and line it up to
start on the first beat of bar 9. Doing this will, of course shorten the
note's length. Just drag the end of the note, to the right, to lengthen it
again.

The track is beginning to sound quite lush now with the addition of those
strings. They hand over to the horns at just the right spot in the song. It
would be nice now if they returned at some point. Maybe they could provide
a back drop to the horns at bar 29. This time, instead of playing the notes,
you're going to draw them, in the Software editor. But firstly, we need to create a region, to contain the notes.

24 Select the Hollywood Strings track and Command-Click at bar 29, to create a new region.

25 Extend the region to the end of bar 33.

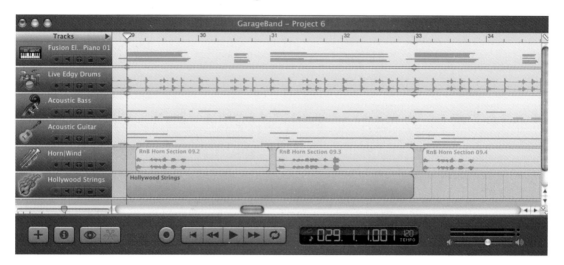

26 Open the advanced editing features in the track editor (click on the tiny triangle, directly above the vertical keyboard).

27 Ensure Notes is selected in the Notes drop down menu.

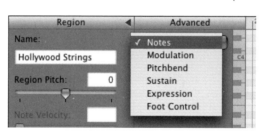

28 Enter the note C4 onto the editor grid. You do this by Command-clicking (the cursor becomes a pencil). Extend it to a length of six beats (one and a half bars).

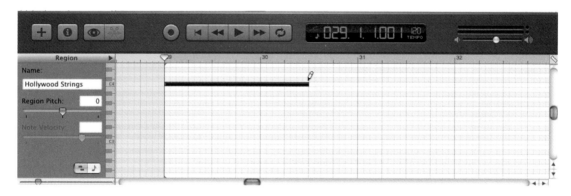

29 Our first string line was played with a velocity of 98, so adjust the new note's velocity value to something similar (use the slider, or type a value in the box).

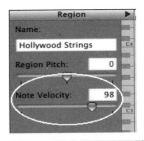

30 Draw another note on the grid, this time, two grid lines down from C4 (A#3). Start it on the third beat of bar 30, so that it plays immediately after the first note. Extend it to a length of two beats (half a bar).

31 Draw a third note on the grid, this time, back at C4. Extend its length to eight beats (two bars).

32 Vary the velocities of each note, for a more natural, realistic sound.

33 Select your newly created Hollywood Strings region (bars 29 – 33) and loop it once, so that it reaches the end of bar 36.

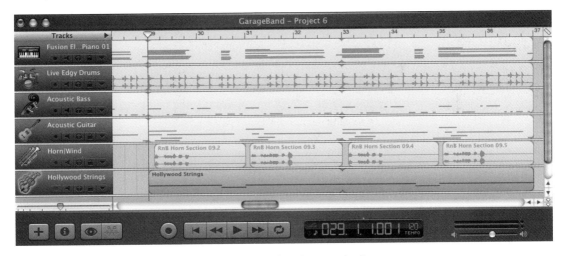

34 Play the song from the beginning and note how the piece gradually builds. Having the strings enter with the guitar (bar 9), before the piano, works well and introduces an air of anticipation, fulfilled when the piano joins in (bar 13). Having them drop out, just as the horns enter (21), helps retain the listener's interest, as does their return, when the horns play a new lick (bar 29).

35 Save this project and name it (project 6) because you will be using it again, as a basis for project 7. You can download my version, for comparison, at http://www.pc-publishing.com/downloads.html..

Assignments

If you don't own a MIDI keyboard the musical typing facility is a great way to play realistic drums, in real time. Create a new GarageBand project and change the default piano track to a rock drum kit (Software Instrument > Drum Kits > Rock Kit), Open the Musical Typing facility. Now practise playing and recording your newly discovered drum kit.

With Octave set to C1 (use keys Z and X to adjust this) the drum kit will be mapped as follows:

A – Kick Drum
S – Snare Drum (tight)
T – Snare Drum (loose)
W – Side Stick
E – Snare Drum Roll
F, G, H, J, K, L – Toms
T – Pedal Hi-hat
Y – Closed Hi-hat
U – Open Hi-hat
O and : – Crash Cymbals
P and ' – Ride Cymbals

- Have some fun and try out the other drum kits in the software menu such as the techno kit. You'll find that, although the mapping is similar, some of the sounds will be very different to a conventional drum kit.
- Try using the musical typing facility to play and record some of the other GarageBand software instruments. You'll find that it works better on some instruments than others.

How to build up a MIDI based drum track using cycle recording.

Like all sequencers, GarageBand provides facilities for cycle recording. By setting up a cycle region you can record a region piece by piece, adding something new on each pass. You can do this with all the software instruments but it's probably most useful when compiling a drum track. Here's how it's done:

1 Create a new song. Choose a comfortable speed. Select a grid setting of 1/8. Ensure the count-in is active.
2 Open the Track Info window and change the default Grand Piano track to a drum kit. Choose any kit you fancy.
3 Press the note C1 (Musical Typing: press A) on your MIDI keyboard and you'll hear a kick drum sound. Press E1, two white notes higher (Musical Typing: T), and you'll hear a snare drum.
4 Set up a four bar cycle and record a four-to-the-bar kick drum beat (or something similar). When you reach the end of the cycle, stop playing but leave GarageBand in record mode.

Tip

It's okay to stop playing and leave GarageBand in record mode. You'll hear the music you've already recorded; none of it will be erased.

5 As the region cycles you can add snare and hi-hat as and when you like. But keep it simple (use nothing smaller than 1/8 notes). Experiment with cymbal crashes and toms as well, if you want. When you're happy, press the spacebar, to stop recording.

6 Play the region back. If it sounds a bit rough, don't worry; just press the Fix Timing button in the track editor.

MIDI keyboards

As mentioned above, the most basic method of playing a software instrument is to use the GarageBand keyboard (press Command-K, to open it). Or better still, use the musical typing facility (press Command-G). But let's face it, playing a virtual keyboard with a mouse or computer keyboard just isn't practical for anything but the most basic recording work. For more professional results you'll need a proper MIDI keyboard and a MIDI interface of some kind.

If you don't already own a MIDI keyboard, companies like M-Audio, Edirol and Yamaha produce dozens of affordable models. The M-Audio Keystation 49e for example features a velocity sensitive keyboard with pitch bend and modulation controls, a volume control slider, foot pedal connections. It also functions as a MIDI interface. A keyboard like this is perfectly adequate for GarageBand.

The M-Audio Keystation 49e is an ideal MIDI keyboard for playing GarageBand's software instruments

Recording and playing software instruments the easy way

Okay, you're now entering the world of MIDI sequencing and all this talk of keyboard playing may be troubling you. Don't worry. It's a common myth that you have to be a good keyboard player to record MIDI tracks. Many accomplished musicians who play instruments such as guitar and saxophone are terrible piano players but that doesn't prevent them recording MIDI tracks in programs like GarageBand.

Maybe you already play a musical instrument. If so, you must have encountered fast passages that you couldn't play the first time round. What did you do? Give up? Of course not. You practised them slowly. Only when the difficult bits were under-the-fingers did you speed them up again (at least that's what you should have done).

The same principles apply when you're playing a GarageBand Software Instrument. If you can't play something fast, just slow the tempo, record the part and then return your song to its original tempo.

Using third party software instruments

You're not just limited to GarageBand's software instruments. If you happen to have any third party Audio Unit instruments on your system you can use those too.

Place them in one of the following locations on your Mac:
HD > Library > Audio > Plug-ins > Components
HD > Users > Home > Library > Audio > Components

Now you can load them into GarageBand. Create a new software instrument track, select it and press Command-I, to open the track info window. In the details section, use the Generator pop-up menu to locate and load your third party software instruments.

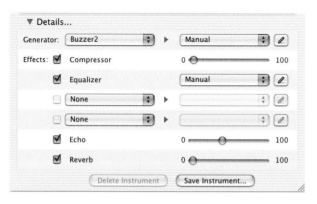

If you're looking for a powerful synth to use with GarageBand, go to http://www.alphakanal.de/snipsnap/space/Buzzer2 and download Buzzer2 – it's brilliant

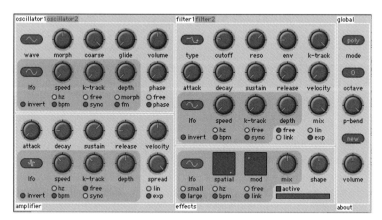

Recording a simple voice-over track

In this project you will:

- Create a blank audio track (Real Instrument track).
- Change a default stereo audio track to a mono audio track.
- Adjust your audio input signal level, to avoid clipping or distortion.
- Record a simple, spoken voice-over vocal track.

So far we've only played back pre-recorded Apple loops on Real Instrument tracks. But, as explained in project 3, GarageBand's Real Instrument tracks are, in fact, audio tracks. And that means that you too can record your own real instruments (guitar, sax or whatever) or vocals onto them. In this project you're going to record your voice. Don't worry; you'll not have to sing anything. All you'll have to do is recite the title of this book, as a voice-over. You can do this using the built-in mic that comes with most Macs.

Follow these steps:

1   Open your finished version of project 6. Alternatively, download my version at http://www.pc-publishing.com/downloads.html. Save a new version and name it project 7.

You'll be recording your voice between bars 21 and 29. It really is very simple but unfortunately, there are a few boring preliminaries. Bear with me.

2   Open GarageBand's Preferences, click the Audio/MIDI tab and ensure that the audio inputs and outputs are correct. If you have an audio interface connected to your computer it appears here, in the pop-up menu, alongside the built-in audio controller. Any MIDI devices you have connected will also show up here.
3   Before you can record your voice you'll need to create a blank audio track (Real Instrument track). From the Track menu, select New Basic Track. A brand new audio track appears called, rather boringly, No Effects (pic overleaf). You can click on the name and change this if you wish. I renamed my audio track Vocals.
4   Open the Track Info window and you'll see that the track is set to record in stereo, by default. Now, if we were planning to record an instrument in stereo, a synthesiser perhaps, we would simply leave the setting as it is;

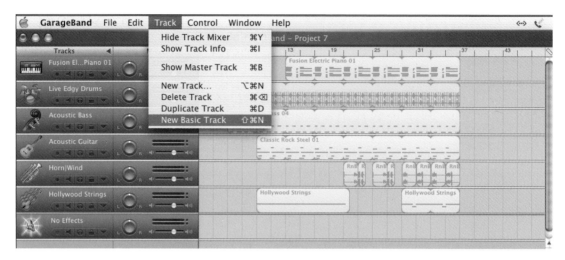

the input channels would display 1/2. But vocals, along with most acoustic instruments, are commonly recorded onto mono tracks.

5   In the Track Info window, choose a mono input from the pop-up menu and turn the monitor option on.

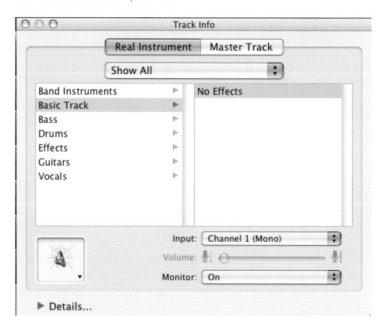

6   Now place yourself at a reasonably close distance to your computer, and sing or speak into the microphone. As you do so, check the signal level in the track mixer. If the signal is too high (hitting red) or too low, use the Volume slider (in the Track Info window, not the slider in the track mixer) to adjust the input level.

If you're using an external audio interface to record audio into GarageBand (as opposed to your Mac's built-in audio facilities) the track info volume slider will be greyed out. Instead, use the software supplied with your audio device, or an external mixer to adjust your audio input signals.

7 Last minute checks - In the GarageBand Preferences, ensure the metronome is turned on. In the Control menu, ensure that Metronome and Count-In are ticked.

Metronome: ⦿ During recording
⠀⠀⠀⠀⠀⠀⠀⠀⠀⠀◯ During playback and recording

You're nearly there. We've reached the exciting bit. You're now going to record your voice, between bars 21 and 29. You'll be reciting the title of this book: 'Keep It Simple With GarageBand'. The best place to do this is in-between the horn notes, which are quite widely spaced apart (see below).

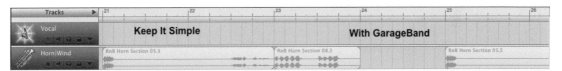

The words 'Keep It Simple' can be spoken just after the initial horn entry, at bar 21. The words 'With GarageBand' fit nicely after the two bursts of rapid successive notes, at the end of bar 23. It doesn't really matter exactly where you place the phrases.

And what happens between bars 25 and 29? Simply repeat the words again; the horns play exactly the same phrase. You could, of course, just record the words once and loop them afterwards. However, recording them twice will introduce variety (remember, repetition and variation are the key to maintaining interest in a composition).

8 Place the Playhead a few bars before bar 21, the point at which you will begin recording. Click the Record button (the red circular button) to start recording. You'll hear the metronome sound a one measure count-in (four beats) before recording starts.
9 Speak the words 'Keep It Simple With GarageBand', at the points suggested above. You'll see a new region appear in the timeline as you record.
10 When you're done (the playhead should be around bar 29, or soon after), click the Play button, to stop the recording.
11 Play back the recording, and if you're not happy with it, do it again. Don't be too fussy though. After all this is just an exercise. If you followed the brief, your finished take should look something like the screen shot overleaf.
12 Save this project and name it (Project 7) because we shall be using it again, as a basis for Project 8. You can download my version, for comparison, at http://www.pc-publishing.com/downloads.html..

Tip

When you're recording your voice over a backing track you don't want the sound from the speakers being re-recorded onto your vocal track as well. To mute the speakers, plug in a decent set of headphones and monitor your performance that way.

Control	Window	Help
✓ Metronome		⌘U
✓ Count In		

Tip

As you record audio in GarageBand, keep an eye on the track level meters, to make sure that the input level isn't 'in the red'. If the red dots next to the level meters light up while you're recording, go into the track info window and use the volume slider to lower the input signal and try recording again.

Assignment

Okay, it's time for you to record something of your own. Obviously, I don't know which instruments you play, if any. But it doesn't matter too much if you can improvise something, nothing difficult, of course. I'll give you some guidelines shortly.

If you play an acoustic instrument or sing, create a new audio track (Real Instrument track) and change it from stereo to mono, as you did in the recently completed project. If you play electric guitar or bass, you will also need to create a mono audio track to record onto. You'll also need a guitar cable (see the guitar cable heading, a little further on in this chapter).

Mute the vocal and horn tracks (click the speaker icon). For this assignment, they are superfluous.

Now record an improvised solo between bars 13 and 37. If you've never played an improvised solo before and you're not sure what to do, just play the notes of this simple pentatonic scale A, C, D, E and G. If you restrict your solo to just these five notes, you can't go wrong, they all fit. Play them in any order you like. Keep it simple and avoid adding any extra notes unless you're confident that they will fit the harmonic structure of the backing. If you're a singer use the same notes to invent a scat solo.

It's a good idea to set up a cycle and practise for a while. As well as getting used to playing or singing your solo, you can check your input signal levels at the same time.

If you don't play an instrument and don't feel comfortable with singing, use the musical typing keyboard to record your solo instead. Create a MIDI track (Software Instrument track) to record onto first. To play the pentatonic scale mentioned above, press these keys: S, D, G, H and K, in any order you like.

Tip

If you're recording via your Mac's built-in audio, it's a good idea to turn off input monitoring (track info window) when you're not playing or singing. With monitoring on, your computer may pick up the output from your speakers and cause feedback (an unpleasant howling noise). That's why monitoring is switched off, by default.

Info

The pentatonic scale is made up of five notes and widely found in folk music around the world. The old Scottish tune, Auld Lang Syne, is a perfect example of its use. It can be easily played using just the black notes on a piano keyboard.

Your Mac's built-in audio facilities – are they good enough?

In the above project you probably used your computer's built-in microphone to record your voice. It's a great feature and all new Macs have one. And, of course, it's perfect for recording vocals and acoustic instruments quickly without the bother of complicated audio interface setups. But let's face it; the built-in microphone isn't up to much, quality-wise. Although you'll find it very useful, it doesn't exactly deliver sonic perfection. And what about electric guitars? You can't record those through the built-in microphone. Clearly then, if you play guitar or maybe just want to improve the quality of your recordings, you'll need some extra equipment.

But of course, you've bought this book because you thought creating and recording music with GarageBand was simple. Don't worry; it needn't be expensive or complicated to go one step further.

So where do you begin? Can you simply plug in a microphone or guitar and begin recording? At it's most basic level yes. After all, GarageBand is an entry-level sequencer and that means you can 'get by' with an entry-level studio set-up using your Mac's limited built-in audio facilities. You see, because GarageBand only supports 16-bit recording, you can also 'get by' without the expense of a top-of-the-range 24-bit audio interface. So, apart from the built-in microphone, just how do you get audio in and out of GarageBand 'on-the-cheap', so to speak?

Microphone cable adaptors

Let's start with microphones. Although you can use the built-in microphone, you'll get better results by connecting a budget microphone directly to your computer's audio in jack. To do this you'll almost certainly need an adaptor of some kind like the GarageBand Microphone Cable from Griffin Technology. That's because all Mac input jacks are 1/8-inch (3.5 mm).

However, although the results are probably going to be a big improvement over recording with the built-in microphone, you should also be aware that the audio mini-jack's prime function is for hooking up consumer products such as CD players. In other words, you'll achieve acceptable but not remarkable results. The audio signal will almost certainly pick up noise from the electrical circuitry within the computer.

Another cost effective way of recording is to use a Griffin iMic, an inexpensive USB adapter. Because it supports both mic and line level input, you can use it to connect both microphones and instruments to your Mac. Also, because USB isolates the audio signal from any noisy electronics in your computer, you'll also get marginally better sound quality.

The audio line in jack is also suitable for recording electrical instruments that output a line level signal such as synthesisers and sound modules. You can also use it to record

The GarageBand Microphone Cable can be used to plug a microphone into your Apple Mac's audio in mini-jack

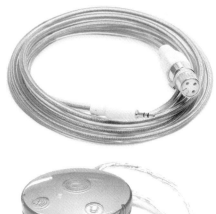

The iMic USB adapter can be used to connect guitars and microphones to Apple Macs

your guitar. But there is a problem. Electric guitars use 1/4-inch size instrument cables and because the Mac audio input is 1/8-inch mini-jack, as with the mic, you'll need an adaptor.

Guitar cables

For recording your guitar, the simplest and probably the cheapest solution is to buy the Griffin GarageBand Guitar Cable. Just plug one end into your guitar and the other into your Mac and it splits the mono guitar signal into the stereo mini-jack. The cable is around 3 metres long.

The GarageBand Guitar Cable - just plug one end into your guitar and the other end into your Mac

Alternatively, you could buy the Monster iStudioLink, a simple 1/4-inch (female) to 1/8-inch stereo mini-plug (male) adapter (www.monstercable. com). Simply plug your guitar into the female plug and the mini-plug into the Mac's audio jack. This neat little adapter can also be used to connect microphones and keyboards to your Mac.

Monster iStudioLink can be used to plug, mics, guitars and keyboards into your Mac

So you see at its simplest level, recording into GarageBand is very affordable (once you've bought the computer that is). For more professional results though it's worth investing in either a FireWire or USB audio interface. If you've got your sights set on a recording contract or maybe even distributing your songs on the Web, this is way to go.

A step further

To make professional quality recordings you need the same kind of audio input and output connections as those found on a professional recording mixer. That means preamps for condenser microphones and high-impedance instrument inputs for connecting guitars and basses. You'll also need direct monitoring facilities for zero latency and a pair of accurate speakers for monitoring your performance and mixing the finished recording. And if you want to access those mouth-watering software instruments included with GarageBand you'll also need a small keyboard and MIDI interface, to play and control them. Sounds like an awful lot of gear to fit on your desktop, doesn't it? Don't worry; it's a lot less complicated than it might appear. In modern computer music studio equipment such as this can easily be accommodated on a desktop.

USB audio and MIDI interfaces

M-Audio manufactures great value-for-money USB and FireWire audio inter-faces (www.m-audio.com) and their least expensive device the Mobilepre USB is designed for location laptop recording. Of course, it works just as well with desktop computers and is perfectly adequate for recording with GarageBand. In fact, all the audio connections you're likely to need are here including two high impedance instrument inputs and two phantom powered mic inputs. However it doesn't include a MIDI interface. If you want to play GarageBand's software instruments a separate MIDI interface is required.

The Mobilepre USB, from M-Audio is perfectly suited for recording with GarageBand

FireWire Audio and MIDI interfaces

FireWire devices are more expensive than their USB counterpart but they're more efficient with superior audio transfer rates. If you're a guitarist the FireWire Solo is an ideal way to get started with GarageBand or Logic. Designed from the ground up as an easy-to-use interface for songwriters to record guitars and vocals it features a 1/4-inch guitar input and a profes-sional XLR microphone input on the front panel. There are also dual line inputs for effects, drum machines and other outboard gear. This model is very much guitar orientated and if you play keyboards you'll need a separate MIDI interface to take advantage of the GarageBand software instruments.

The M-Audio FireWire Solo was designed specially for guitar players

Microphones

Most audio interfaces feature at least one XLR connection and a preamp. There's a good reason for this; they can be used to connect condenser micro-phones. They'll accept dynamic microphones too but condenser types are usually chosen for recording vocals and acoustic instruments.

Budget priced multi-pattern studio microphones like the Samson CO3 are ideal for recording vocals and acoustic instruments in the project studio

If you're going to buy one just one microphone (and if you're working alone, that's probably all you need) get either a Shure SM58 (dynamic mic) or a condenser model. Top-of-the-range condenser microphones are very expensive but companies like Samson Audio manufacture excellent budget models. Their CO3 model for example is a multi-pattern condenser microphone developed specifically for project studio use.

But why a condenser? Condenser microphones are very sensitive with a good high frequency response. In common with the very best studio microphones the Samson CO3 can be switched between different pickup patterns; Cardoid, Omni and Figure 8. Cardoid is the most commonly used setting and being unidirectional rejects sounds on either side of the microphone in favour of sounds directly in front of it; useful for recording a solo vocalist. The Omni pickup pattern captures sound from all directions, useful for recording ensembles. The Figure 8 pattern picks up sound directly at the front and back of the microphone, useful for duets and backing vocals.

Dynamic microphones are more robust than condenser types and a good one such as the classic Shure SM58 can be used to close-mic just about anything with surprisingly good results. They're also good for recording vocals.

Headphones and speakers

A frequently asked question: Can I use headphones instead of speakers when recording and mixing my music? The answer is yes, but it's not wholeheartedly recommended. Headphones are fine for monitoring your performance while you're recording but for mixing the tracks afterwards you really need a couple of decent speakers with a flat frequency response. In fact you should buy the best you can afford because accuracy is paramount when mixing.

Fortunately good budget reference monitors are becoming increasingly common. The Resolv range from Samson Audio for example are good value for money. The Resolv 60a powered speakers produce a full sound with a transparent mid-range. M-Audio also manufactures reasonably priced reference monitors called the Studiophile range.

A pair of studio reference monitors like the Samson Resolv 6a will help you create accurate mixes

Unlike speakers, accurate headphones are not so critical. But there are one or two factors you should take into consideration before purchasing. A closed design is better than an open type. Why? Because when you're overdubbing vocals or whatever, you don't want sound leaking from your 'phones. This can be picked up and recorded along with your performance.

It's not the drastic issue that some people make out and can even be quite effective but even so, it's best avoided and can prove problematic when it comes to mixing. A long lead that connects to just one side is also preferable for avoiding entanglement with instruments and so on. As well as being powerful and comfortable to wear, the AKG K55 studio headphones fit the bill. They're also very reasonably priced.

These AKG K55 headphones are a closed-back design, just what you need for zero leakage when overdubbing vocals.

Audio MIDI Setup (AMS)

Before using an audio interface you'll need to configure the input and output connections in the OS X Audio MIDI Setup (AMS).

1 Install any drivers that came with your equipment.
2 Ensure that your audio interface is connected to your Mac.
3 Open the AMS. You'll find it under Applications > Utilities > Audio MIDI Setup.

4 Select the Audio Devices tab at the top of the dialogue box.
5 In the System Settings area, select your audio interface in the Default Input pop-up menu. If you don't have a third-party audio interface and you're going to use the audio-in jack on your Mac, choose Built-in Audio.

6 By way of a check, open the OS X Sound System Preferences as well and select the Input page. Your device will appear here too (along with any other audio devices you have connected). In fact both the Sound and AMS windows interact. Change the settings in one window and the settings will be reflected in the other. If you're going to use your Mac's analogue audio inputs ensure that Line In is selected in the Sound window.

7 In the AMS window, select your audio interface in the Default Output
   pop-up menu. Leave the System Output set to Built-in audio controller.
   That way you'll not hear the system bleeps through your audio interface
   but through your computer's speaker(s).

Before using your MIDI devices you'll need to configure a setup in the OS X
Audio MIDI Setup (AMS).

1 Install any drivers that came with your equipment.
2 Ensure that your MIDI interface is connected to your Mac.
3 Open the AMS. You'll find it under Applications > Utilities > Audio MIDI
   Setup.
4 All connected MIDI devices will show up here (the greyed-out IAC driver
   enables you to configure different setups for different applications). If
   their drivers have been installed correctly, other unconnected devices will
   also appear here (but like the IAC, they'll be greyed out).
5 To add a MIDI keyboard controller (or any other MIDI device) click the
   Add Device icon. A new external device icon appears.
6 Click on the new device's output and drag a virtual cable to the MIDI
   interface's input.

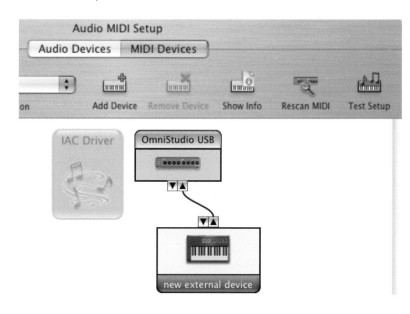

Gating and compressing your vocal track

In this project you will:

- Learn how, why and when to use the GarageBand Gate (noise gate).
- Learn how, why and when to use the GarageBand Compressor.
- Gender-bend your vocal track using one of the many GarageBand audio-processing effects.

In Project 7, you recorded a 'voice-over' on an audio track. The actual quality of your recording is, obviously, unknown to me.

If you achieved a healthy input level, without any peaking, your recording probably sounds fine. Even so, in most cases, a vocal recording can be improved upon with the aid of some careful processing, to make it sound truly professional.

Listen carefully to your recording again. Were there any background noises picked up, in the silent passages between your spoken words? – A distant door closing or maybe a muffled cough. It's surprising how noises that we don't ordinarily notice, can sometimes turn up on our home studio recordings. Even if your recording is totally free from extraneous noise there is probably some evidence of breathing and possible body movement, somewhere between the words. Listen to my version (at http://www.pc-publishing.com/downloads.html) and you'll hear the sound of breathing. Listen really hard and you'll notice, too, that the horns have leaked onto the track, although very faintly.

How do we get rid of this unwanted noise? We could, of course, edit the noise out manually, which in this case, admittedly, wouldn't take long. In fact, I've trimmed the beginning of my vocal region, to hide an audible intake of breath. But if this was a longer piece, manual editing could take ages. Fortunately, there's a quicker way that provides instant results. We use GarageBand's built-in noise gate.

Follow these steps:

1 Open your finished version of Project 7. Alternatively, download my version at http://www.pc-publishing.com/downloads.html. Save a new version, this time, as Project 8.
2 Solo your recently recorded vocal track (click on the headphone icon in the track mixer) and turn up the volume, so that you can scrutinise the recording.

3   Make sure the track is soloed. Then with the vocal track selected, click the Track Info button or double-click the track's header, to open the Track Info window.
4   Click the Details triangle. A new pane is revealed containing the track effects settings.
5   Click the Gate checkbox.

6   Move the gate's slider back to the zero position. Then gradually move
    the slider to the right until all the background sounds in between the
    words 'Keep It Simple' are eliminated. Go too far and you'll cut out some
    of the words (gate chattering); slide it to the maximum position and the
    voice will disappear entirely. Experiment and find the optimum position.

When recording the human voice and many acoustic instruments, maintaining a constant input level can be a bit of a problem. It's more of a concern
with a sung performance than a spoken one, but even so, listen to your
recording again and you'll probably hear that some words were spoken louder than others. This is easily fixed with the use of compression.

7   Ensure the vocal track is soloed. Then return to the Track Info box and
    click the Compressor check box.
8   Gradually move the slider to the right, until your vocal performance is
    pretty even sounding – so that you can hear all the words at much the
    same level.

9   Disable the solo feature and check your voice against the other tracks.
    Are the words coming through loud and clear? If not, apply some more
    compression. You may have to raise the track mixer volume slider slightly
    or lower the other instruments. But don't get into a heavy duty mixing
    section just yet. We'll deal with that in a separate project.

Now for a bit of fun. There's a whole range of GarageBand effects that we
could use to process and enhance your voice but we'll leave that until the
mix. However, to get an idea of how to apply them, you're now going 'gen-
der bender' your voice.

10 Ensure the vocal track is soloed. Then return to the Track Info box and
    select the Vocal Transformer effect from one of the two Effects pop-up
    menus.

11 Depending upon your sex, choose either the Female to Male or the Male
    to Female preset from the adjacent Preset pop-up menu. To get at the
    effect parameters, click on the Edit button (the pencil icon). To get the
    effect just right, you'll have to experiment a little with the two sliders. I'll

leave you to be the judge of the effectiveness of this particular GarageBand effect. It's good fun though, whatever the result.

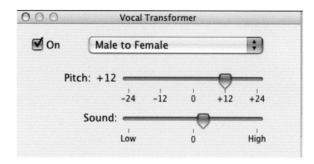

Okay, enough of that. Disable the vocal transformer and save the project. Name it (project 8) because we shall be using it again, as a basis for project 9. You can download my version, for comparison, at http://www.pc-publishing.com/downloads.html.

Assignments

In the same way that you used the Vocal Transformer in project 8, experiment with other effects on the vocal track. Track Echo is a good one. Some the effects will work well. Some, like Distortion are unsuitable for vocals. Try adding the Flanger to the acoustic guitar track. You'll find that guitars lend themselves particularly well to effects treatment. Also, try a few effects on the horns. Have fun, experiment as much as you like but don't save anything (not as project 8 anyway because it's going to be used as a basis for project 9).

More about gates and compressors

A noise gate (sometimes called an expander) removes unwanted noises during gaps in the audio. When the input level falls below a predetermined threshold the gate reduces the gain. In other words, when a track's instrument stops playing for a moment the gate kicks in and turns down the volume. Any noise you or your instrument might have made when you ceased playing – rustling lyric sheets, guitar hums and crackles, foot-tapping, even breathing – can be removed during the pause.

To use GarageBand's gate, slowly move the slider to the right until any unwanted noise on the track disappears. If the gate begins chopping off notes and vocal syllables move the slider back a little.

A compressor works as an automatic volume control, turning down the volume when the audio is too loud and turning it up when it's too quiet. Why should you need that?

Suppose you've recorded a vocal. On listening back you discover that your voice varied considerably in volume over the course of the song. The high notes were sung more vigorously and as a result, were recorded louder. They tend to leap out of the mix. The lower notes were sung with less intensity and the recorded signal is rather low. They tend to get buried in the mix.

Tip

Adding effects to your tracks quickly uses up valuable computer processing power. To free up valuable CPU, lock those tracks that you are not currently processing (click the padlock icon). For example, if you are adding a couple of processor intensive effects to your vocal track, lock all the other tracks. GarageBand will temporally render those tracks – and their individual processor settings – to your hard drive, as audio files. If you need to work on one of the locked tracks, simply unlock it.

You could, of course, ride the faders (constantly adjust them while you're mixing), to obtain an even signal. But that's a difficult task even on a hardware console, let alone using a mouse in GarageBand. You could also set up an automated volume curve but finding and rectifying all the uneven spots is a time consuming task.

A compressor does all this for you, automatically. When the input level exceeds a predetermined threshold the compressor reduces the gain. When the input signal is below the threshold, it's unaffected.

Compression is also used creatively, to beef up guitar, bass and drums in rock music. Dance music producers also use heavy doses of compression on bass and drums, to get that floor-quaking effect.

GarageBand's compressor is very simple to operate. Just use the slider to increase the compression effect.

Tip

On lead vocals and acoustic instruments, use the compression slider sparingly, adding just enough to make the vocal sit nicely in the mix. Too much compression can spoil an otherwise exciting performance.

Improving the bass line (MIDI editing)

Apart from extending your *Keep It Simple With GarageBand* theme tune further, which isn't really the point of this book, there's not a great deal left to do here. You're fast approaching the mixing stage now. But before you get into that you're going to make a couple of changes to the bass track, which is MIDI based. The work will take place in the track editor.

In this project you will:

- View the bass line as MIDI data, in the track editor.
- View the bass line as musical notation, in the track editor.
- Alter the pitch of the notes in the track editor, to create a new, improved bass line.
- Draw pitchbend controller information in the track editor, to create a bass glissando.

Follow these steps:

1 Open your finished version of Project 8. Alternatively, download my version at http://www.pc-publishing.com/downloads.html. Save a new version and name it Project 9.
2 Set up a four bar cycle between bars 5 and 9.
3 Select and solo the Acoustic Bass track.

Have a listen. Rhythmically, this is a good bass line but only two notes are used; C and G. In essence, there's nothing wrong with that, but this one has limited note movement, within a narrowly confined range – C3 down to G2. Melodically, this is rather unimaginative and the loop tends to sound monotonous after a while. The screen shot (top of next page) shows the bass line viewed graphically, in the grid based editor. You're now going to look at the data another way, as music notation.

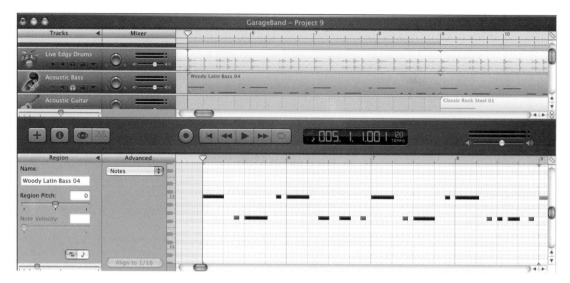

4   Open the track editor and click on the tiny note icon (just above the zoom slider).

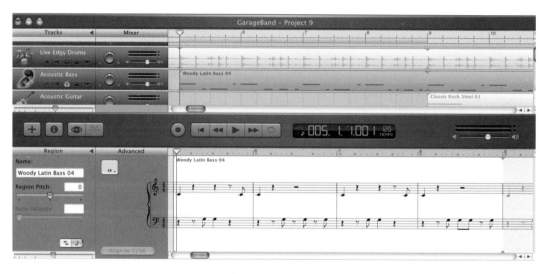

The graphic view will change to standard musical notation. Unfortunately the display is only available as double stave piano style notation and the bass line jumps from one to the other. It's a rather confusing picture but if you read music you'll notice that the two bass notes are conveniently displayed on the two separate staves – C2, on the top one and G2 on the lower.

As mentioned above the note range here is strictly limited. To open things up a little, you're going to move the seventh note in the loop, down by an octave. You can do this both in either the notation view or the grid view.

5. Assuming you're using the graphic display, simply grab the seventh note of the loop and drag it down to G1. You can do exactly the same thing in the notation display, if you prefer.

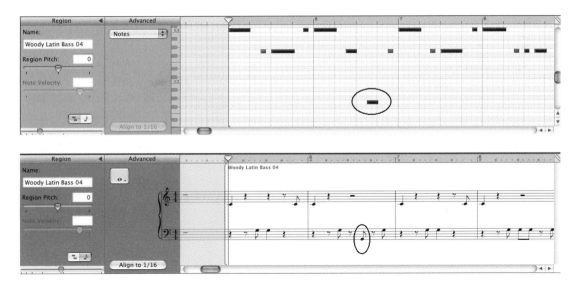

Play it through. That's a lot better but there's more to do

6   Move the 12th and 13th notes in the loop up a musical fifth, from C3 to
    G3.

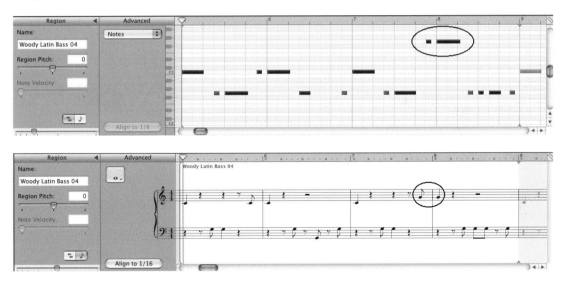

   Play it through. It's better now. However, you can make it even more
interesting by introducing a small slide up to the newly changed 13th note.
String bass players often do this in real life.

7   If the editor is displaying musical notation, change it to the graphic view.
8   In the Advanced section of the editor, choose Pitchbend, from the pop-up
    menu. You're going to draw pitch bend information onto the grid that
    corresponds with the 13th note of the loop, dead on the first beat of bar 8.
9   Command-clicking will turn your mouse cursor into a pencil. With the

pencil, enter a control point at bar 8, a little way below the horizontal green line that indicates zero. The note will now start a little below pitch.

10 Enter another control point, an 1/8 note later, but this time, dead on the green horizontal line.

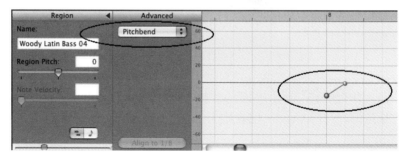

11 Play it through. Notice how the note now slides up to the correct pitch. This effect is known in musical terms as a glissando.

12 Save the project. Name it (project 9) because you will be using it again, as a basis for project 10. You can download my version, for comparison, at http://www.pc-publishing.com/downloads.html.

Assignment

Return to your saved version of project 8. Using the same techniques as above (project 9, steps 5 and 6) re-write the bass line, to your liking. Add pitch bend information if you wish. For more variety, try altering and lengthening some of the notes (see 'More about editing notes in the Track Editor', a little further on in this chapter). If you're feeling adventurous, go to work on the acoustic guitar track as well. If you save your work, be sure to name it something other than project 8, just in case you need to return to it.

More about editing MIDI controller data in the track editor

Three types of MIDI controller can be recorded and edited in Garage Band: modulation (think vibrato), pitch bend (think note bending on a guitar or wind instruments) and sustain (the same effect as holding down a piano's sustain pedal - the notes ring on). To record this data fluently you need a MIDI controller. Pitch bend and modulation are transmitted using a controller wheel, commonly found on synths and MIDI keyboards. You select the type from the Display pop-up menu, in the Advanced section.

When Pitchbend is selected any pitch bend data that you recorded is displayed on the grid as an envelope. Anything above zero raises the pitch. Anything below zero lowers the pitch. You can alter the curve by selecting and dragging the nodes.

When Modulation is selected any modulation data that you recorded is displayed on the grid as an envelope. Modulation is represented numerically (0-127). The higher the value, the more intense the effect.

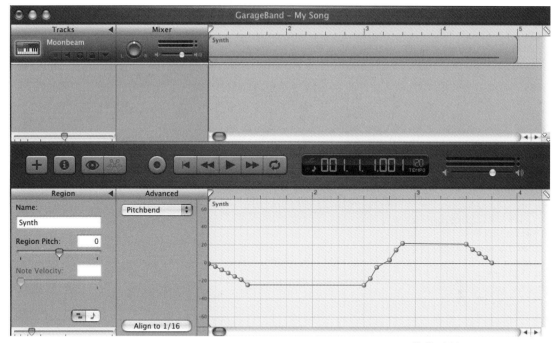

Pitchbend data

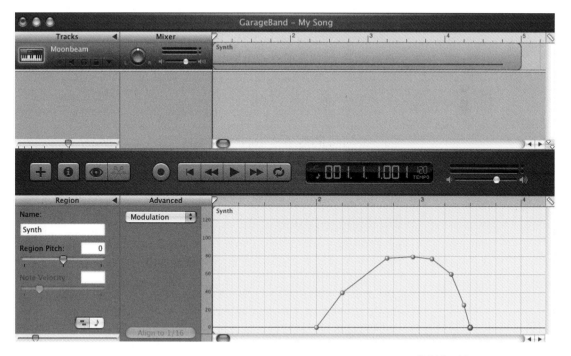

Modulation data

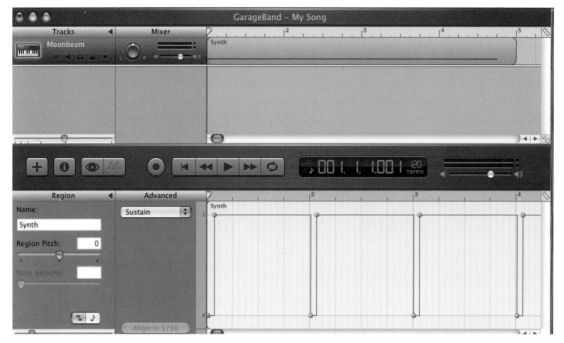

Sustain data

When Sustain is selected a single node represents either on or off. In the picture below sustain is turned on in bar 1 and is turned off at bar 2.

More about editing notes in the Track Editor

While the structure of a piece of music can be edited on the timeline, detailed editing of a region's contents can only be carried out in the track editor.

When you open the track editor with a Software Instrument region selected the MIDI data is always displayed graphically, on a piano roll style grid. Pitch is represented vertically (piano keyboard, on the left-hand side) and time horizontally (the beat ruler, above the grid). Six types of data can be displayed on this grid which you select from the Display pop-up menu, in the Advanced section.

When Notes is selected (default setting), any notes you've played can be seen on the grid. How they are displayed is determined by the grid selection you make, which is independent from the timeline's grid settings. The timing can be fixed (quantised) according to the grid setting and is a handy feature for bringing inaccurately played notes into line. But it can also be used creatively, to inject swing into jazzier styles of music. To hear the effect: Record a few 1/8 notes, choose a grid setting of 1/8 Swing Heavy (or Light), select the entire region and press the 'Align to 1/8' button in the Advanced area.

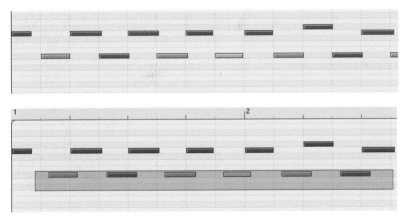

Notes in the Track Editor before applying Swing

Notes in the Track Editor after Swing is applied – every other 1/8 note is moved to the right (played back slightly later)

Changing a note's length – you can alter the length of notes (or groups of notes, using Shift) on the grid by dragging their ends, to the right. To alter the pitch of an entire region, firstly select it in the timeline and then use the Transpose slider, in the track editor. It has a range of three octaves up and down, either side of zero.

Changing a note's pitch – to alter the pitch of a note (or groups of notes, using Shift) all you need do is drag the note(s) up or down on the grid.

Changing a note's volume – you can alter the volume of individual notes (or groups of notes, using Shift) with the velocity slider. The value (1-127) reflects how hard a note is struck on the keyboard.

Tip

If you alter the notes in a looped region, all instances of the loop will be changed as well. If this is not want you want to do, use the split command to isolate just the notes you intend altering.

The mix

You've reached the mixing stage, where the individual tracks are balanced and treated in order to make up a pleasing and satisfying whole. The end result can then be exported to iTunes as a two-track stereo audio file.

Follow these steps:

1 Open your finished version of Project 9. Alternatively, download my version at http://www.pc-publishing.com/downloads.html. Save a new version and name it Project 10.

Different people approach 'mixing' in different ways, depending on the type of productions they happen to be working on. This project is fairly conventional and for that reason I'm going to adopt a traditional studio engineer's approach. Typically, they would be mixing this project using a recording console, complete with a set of vertical faders, as opposed to GarageBand's horizontal sliders. And one of the first things they would do is pull all the track faders down, so…

2 In the track mixer, one by one, drag all the volume sliders to the left. This will effectively mute the playback of the entire song. Test this by pressing the play button.

For now, leave the master volume slider at 0.0 db. If it's not there already you can set it 0.0 db by option clicking, on your computer keyboard.

The drum track

3 Set up a cycle region between bars 5 and 9.

4 Select and play the drum track. While the track is playing, gradually raise the drum track volume slider until you achieve a decent level, without going into the red. Around – 7 db will probably be about right.

Now this is a well-recorded drum loop and there's not a great deal we need do to improve it. But we can tweak it a little, to suit our own personal taste.

5 Open the Track info box and click on the Details triangle. You'll see a range of track effects here.

Now a professional engineer usually starts with a clean slate without using flattering effects like reverb and echo. These can be added later. At this stage you need a clean signal and these types of effects will only cloud your judge-ment. Gates, compressors and EQ, however, are not really effects but signal processors. At the outset of a mix these are very useful engineering tools.

So what's the best order to use these processors and effects? Well, in most cases, in the order laid out here in the track info window, from top to bottom. No intrusive noises exist on the drum track. Therefore you don't need the gate. Start with the compressor.

6 Un-tick all the boxes except for the Compressor.
7 Play the cycled section, listen carefully, and apply just a tiny amount of compression. This will define the kick drum more clearly, making it sound just a little tighter. The snare drum is affected in a similar way. You can A/B the effect by turning the compressor off and on, using the tick-box.

Turning on and using the compressor will probably raise the drum track vol-ume a little. If that's happening, and the meter is hitting the danger area, lower the volume, to compensate.

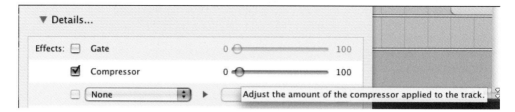

Of course, our studio engineer's console would have an array of EQ con-trols to fine-tune each drum. But as you are working with a complete drum kit mix, this work has mostly been done for you. But you can make a few EQ adjustments without drastically altering the existing character of the sound.

8 Switch on the Equalizer (tick the box) and choose the Add Sharpness preset from the pop-up menu (to the right). This will add a little more 'snap' to the snare drum.

9 At this point, you may like to experiment with the equalizer yourself. To edit my chosen preset, click on the tiny pencil icon, just to the right of the equaliser preset pop-up menu. The Equalizer's controls will appear.

It's important to remember that on a professional multi-track recording our engineer would normally have the drum kit spread over several tracks. For example, kick drum on track 1, the snare drum on track 2 and so on. However, we are working on a pre-mixed drum loop and what you can do with the equalizer here is limited. Whatever changes you make will affect the entire kit, not just an individual drum. Trade-offs will have to be made.

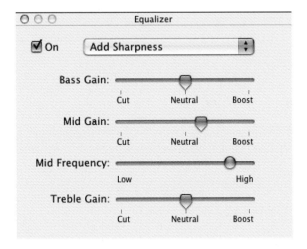

The snare drum occupies the middle frequency area of the audio spectrum and the two controls you'll be using here are the Mid Frequency and Mid Gain sliders. Which particular frequency is affected depends upon the Mid Frequency slider position. Move it to the right, to pinpoint the higher mid frequency ranges. Move it to the left to find the lower mid frequencies. The Mid Gain slider is used to either cut or boost the chosen frequency. At the moment the Add Sharpness preset is set to slightly boost the higher mid frequencies.

When you've finished experimenting return the Equalizer to either the factory Manual preset or the Add Sharpness preset. Otherwise, you might go off at a tangent to this project. You can experiment as much as you like afterwards, of course.

Your drum track info details should now look something like this:

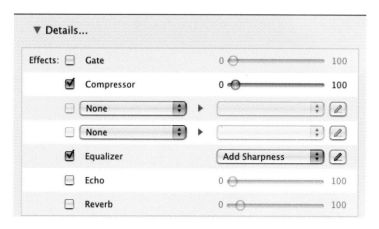

10 Make a final check that the track volume level is under control and we'll move on.

The acoustic bass track

11 Select the bass track and play the cycled section. As you did with the drums, gradually raise the track volume. Listen carefully, to achieve an equal balance between the bass and drums, neither one dominating the other.

At this point our professional recording engineer will want to listen to and scrutinize the bass track in isolation, so...

12 Solo the bass track (click on the headphone icon).
13 Open the track info window and un-tick all the boxes except for the Equalizer.

You're going to use the track equaliser to boost the bass frequencies a little. Start with the Bass Boost preset. This time, at first glance anyway, it appears that you only have a single slider (Bass Gain) to worry about. However cutting or boosting the lower mid frequencies will also affect the bass. Experiment by all means. But when you're finished, just as you did when treating the drums, return the Equalizer either to the factory Manual preset or the Bass Boost preset, just to make sure that we're both working and listening along similar lines.

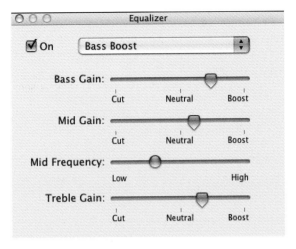

Info

Using EQ to boost any frequencies, not just the bass ones, will result in louder audio signals. So if you've settled for the Bass Boost preset then you'll most likely have to reduce the bass track's volume a little.

14 Un-solo the bass track and recheck the balance between the bass and drums. If the bass is too loud reduce the track's volume.

Your bass track info window should now look something like this:

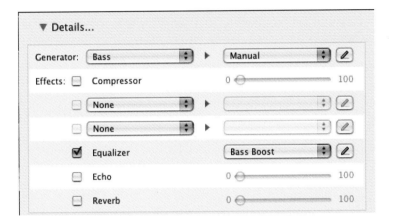

The acoustic guitar track

15 Select the guitar track. The guitar makes its entry at bar 9, so...
16 Set up a cycle region between bars 9 and 13. This is easily done by grabbing the existing yellow cycle marker and moving it along by four bars.
17 Play the cycled selection and gradually increase the track volume until the guitar is evenly balanced against the bass and drums.
18 Solo the guitar track.
19 Open the guitar track info window and un-tick all the boxes except for the Compressor.
20 Apply a moderate amount of compression to the guitar track. Doing so will help raise the volume of the quieter notes in this loop.

This is a nice enough acoustic guitar sound that for a solo, unaccompanied piece, would be very acceptable. But once it's mixed in with the rhythm section, including the electric piano, it's likely to get lost. Why not try adding a chorus effect, to beef it up a bit?

21 Directly beneath the Compressor there's a second Effects slot. It should be empty at the moment. Select the GarageBand Chorus effect and apply the Medium Chorus preset. This will provide the guitar with a reasonably fat chorus sound, without going over the top.

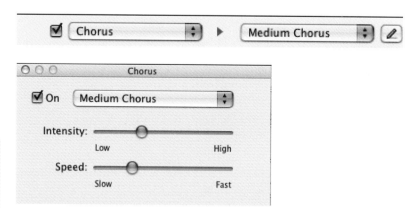

22 Un-solo the guitar track and listen to the chorused guitar in context with the bass and drums. In my opinion that's a big improvement. Of course, it's all a matter of taste. You may prefer it untreated. But for now, go with it. That way we'll be on track together. If necessary, re-adjust the guitar track volume before moving on.

Your guitar track info window should now look something like this:

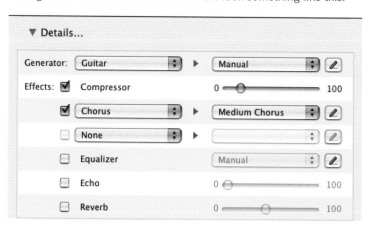

The electric piano track

23 Select the electric piano track. The piano makes its entry at bar 13, so…
24 Set up a cycle region between bars 13 and 17.
25 Play the cycled section and gradually increase the track volume until the
   piano is evenly balanced against the guitar, bass and drums.
26 Solo the electric piano track.
27 Open the electric piano track info window and un-tick all the boxes
   except for the Compressor and the Phaser effect.

As with the guitar, some gentle compression here works fine. But to be frank,
it doesn't make a great deal of difference whether it's on or off. It's up to
you. The Phaser though is vital. If you turn off the Phaser effect the juiciness
disappears from the piano altogether. You'll be left with a thin sounding raw
electric piano sound. Try it and listen for yourself (remember though to turn
it back on again).

The Fusion Electric Piano loop should have loaded with a manual preset
that looks like the picture below.

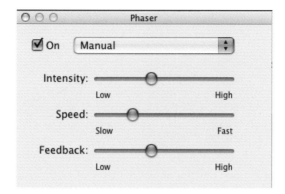

This preset works very well. Experiment with the others and invent your
own by all means. But be careful because too much 'swirl' (listen to the
Surrounding preset to hear what I mean), will interfere with the brass and
vocal overdub, later in the mixing process.

28 Un-solo the piano track, to see how it all fits together. Make any
   adjustments to the track volume that you think necessary.

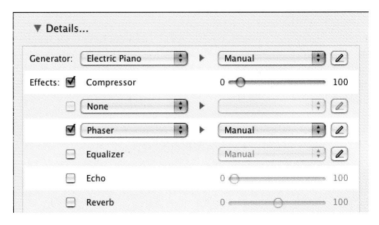

Your electric piano track info window should look something like the above. Just for reference, at this point my track levels looked like this:

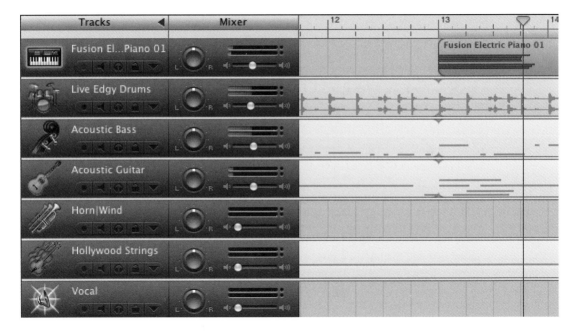

The horn track

At this point you could work on the strings, after all they make their first entry at bar 9 and you are already at bar 13. So why have they been left out? Well, they're really just a backdrop to the horns and the vocal. Until these are sorted out first it's hard to make an objective judgement about the tone of the strings, whether they need effects, and just how loud they should be. It's better to work on the horns next.

29 Set up a cycle region between bars 21 and 29.
30. Select the horn track and gradually raise the track fader to achieve a sensible balance between the horns and the rhythm section instruments. When it sounds good…

31 Solo the horn track.

32 Open the horn track info window and un-tick all the boxes. You will now hear the horns completely dry. In all likelihood they were recorded in a soundproof studio without any natural reverberation. And that's just how you want them because you can now add just the right amount of reverb yourself, to suit the overall character of the project.

Info – Wet or dry? Some reverb blurb

Adding reverb to a track is dead easy, you just turn it on (tick the Reverb box) and move the slider to the right until it sounds nice. You've probably already tried this at some point yourself anyway. But do you know where the reverb is coming from? Did you know that you could use different types reverbs, halls, rooms, and even cathedral types? Read the Send and Return (Master) Effects info box before proceeding further.

Info – Send and return (master) effects

Each track in a GarageBand project has it's own signal path. Insert an effect into a track's signal path and only the audio on that particular track will be affected; no others. However, as you've probably already discovered, inserting effects uses lots of computer processing power. As reverb is commonly used on several tracks in a project it makes sense to use it as a 'send effect'. In other words, reverb is inserted once, in the master track, and made available (sent) to all the other tracks. Only one reverb type is sent at a time. But generally speaking that makes sense because all the instruments in the project are treated with the same acoustic space - halls, cathedrals, rooms and so on.

OK, I'm assuming that you've read the Send and Return (Master) Effects info box and that you now fully understand the concept of send-and-return so...

33 From the horn track info window, open the Master Track info window (click the tab, at the top of the window).

34 Turn off all the effects in the master track except Reverb (un-tick the boxes).

35 From the Reverb pop-up menu choose the Medium Hall global preset.

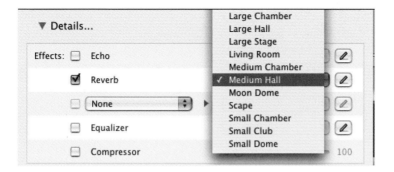

There are lots of other more exotic reverbs on offer here. But it's important to remember that this is a global reverb setting that will be used later to treat some of the other instruments in your project as well. A medium hall setting will provide the required natural ambience.

36 Return to the Real Instrument window (click the tab, at the top of the window) and turn on the Reverb (tick the box). Apply a moderate amount of the effect, using the slider. If the horns begin to sound like they're playing in the distance, you've gone too far. Aim for a natural hall sound.

In my opinion (and I'm a horn player) these horns would benefit from some mid frequency boost, to make them cut through just a bit more. They're a touch mushy, to my taste anyway.

37 Turn on the Equalizer (tick the box) and select the Add Sharpness preset. Doing so will make the horns sound brighter, and in my opinion, more natural sounding. If you don't agree, just leave them as they were and turn of the equalizer. To be frank, it's not going to make a great deal of difference either way.

38 Un-solo the track and make any necessary volume adjustments.

That's it as far the horns are concerned. All they needed was a little presence. Your horn track info window should look something like this:

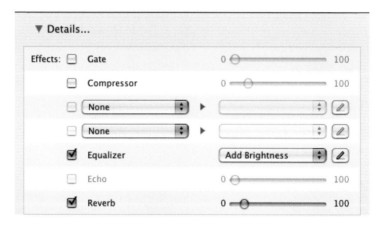

The vocal track

The voice-over track starts at much the same place as the horns so we'll deal with that next.

39 Set up a cycle region to encompass your vocal performance.

40 Select and play the vocal track. Gradually raise the volume until your voice is loud enough to be heard above the backing. Exactly how loud is up to you. But it should be loud enough, at least, for the words to be clearly heard.

41 Solo the vocal track.

42 Open the vocal track info window. If you recorded your own vocal (in project 7) then you will have probably already treated your voice with either the Gate or the Compressor (in project 8). This will be reflected in the track info box. Leave those settings as they.

43 Un-tick all the effect boxes (except your gate and compressor settings), including Reverb. You'll deal with that shortly.

44 At this point you may need to alter the tonal aspects of your voice with the Equalizer. What you do, of course, depends upon the individual characteristics of your voice. Try selecting a preset, Vocal Presence, for example, and take it from there. Un-solo the track frequently, to check that the changes you make fit well with the overall sound of the track.

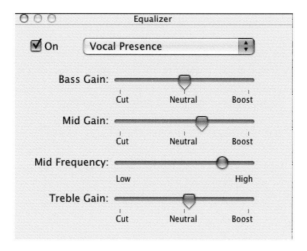

45 Now activate the Reverb slot and apply just a small amount. Just as with the horns, too much will make your voice sound very distant. Use it sparingly.

46 Un-solo the vocal track and make any necessary volume adjustments. You may have to return to the track info window, to make further equalisation settings.

Your vocal track info window should now look something like this:

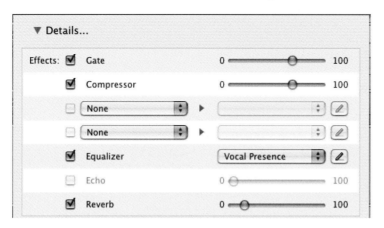

The string track

47 The strings make an entry at Bar 9, play a single long note and drop out again around about bar 22. So set up a cycle to encompass that long note.

48 Select and play the string track. Gradually raise the string volume until it can just be heard behind the other instruments. The strings are going to provide a backdrop and mustn't be too loud.

49 Open the string track info window. The Hollywood Strings preset uses the Equalizer and Reverb (disable any other effects that happen to be ticked).

50 If necessary, adjust the reverb setting. Compared to the other tracks, you can afford to be a little more generous with the reverb on the strings. We want them in the background, audible but not intrusive. A modest amount of reverb will help to achieve this. No other effects are needed on this track.

51 Return to the string track and play the song. The strings enter rather abruptly, don't you think? Real players however are more likely to ease their way in here.

52 On the string track, click the small triangle that opens up the volume curve controls.

In the timeline, you'll notice that a horizontal line has appeared on the string track. This represents the current volume fader setting. In the picture below this is set to 0.dB.

53 Click on the volume curve at bar 11. A control point appears. This action also activates the Track Volume control and turns on the blue indicator light.

54 Scroll back to bar 9 and create another control point.

55 Drag the new control point, downwards, as far as it will go.

56 Locate the very first control point on the string track (bar 1) and drag it
downwards, as far as it will go.

The strings are now effectively muted when the song starts, will enter at bar
nine and fade up to full volume at bar 11.

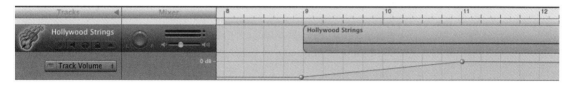

57 Using the same technique, create a downward fade, a couple of bars or
so before the strings finish playing that long note.

58 The strings enter again at bar 29. Once again create an upward fade.
But this time, make the fade-up shorter, about a bar long. There's more
going on this time around.

After you have finished, your string track volume curve should look something like the picture below. Your own volume settings, of course, will be
slightly different. I used a maximum volume setting of 0.dB for visual clarity.
In reality, it was lower than this.

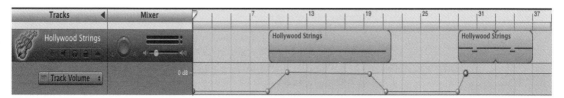

Pan Settings

As I'm sure you are aware, GarageBand outputs audio signals in stereo. In
other words, there are two signals. One is sent to the left speaker and the
other to the right speaker. If the volume level output of a particular track,
let's say the guitar, is louder on the left than the right, then the guitar itself
will sound as if it's coming from the left speaker. The louder the left channel,
the further to the left the guitar will be placed in the stereo picture. This is
referred to as panning. The guitar is panned to the left.

Now try this:

59 Select the guitar track and set the volume/pan curve to Track Pan.

60 At bar 1, drag the pan control point downwards, as far as it will go.

61 Play all the tracks together and you'll hear the guitar emanating from the left speaker only. Leave it there for the moment.

62 Select the electric piano track and using the same technique, pan the piano hard to right (drag the control point upwards, as far as it will go).

63 Play all the tracks together and you'll now hear the guitar, hard left, and piano, hard right. You've created a stereo picture. The piece now sounds much fuller.

64 Okay, you've got the idea. Now, if you want, move the guitar and piano just a little way towards the centre. Move them just a little way and you'll not disturb the newly created stereo image.

When both the stereo audio signals are set at equal volume levels, what you hear will sound as if it's in the middle of the audio spectrum. This is obviously an illusion. After all, we know that it's really coming from both sides. But it's a very convenient illusion because we can leave the other instruments and the vocal in the middle.

The bass part is almost always left in the centre as is the bass drum. In this case all the drums and cymbals are on a single track so we leave them in the centre. Vocals are traditionally panned to the centre also.

The horns could be panned to the left or the right but I've left them in the centre, for the sake of simplicity. And, to begin with anyway, they take the lead between bars 29 and 37.

The strings provide a backdrop and can also remain in the centre. The added reverb will provide a degree of stereo spread here. In fact, now is a good time to check the reverb level, on the string track. Increase the level, if necessary.

65 Play the entire piece through, listening carefully. Avoid having the overall volume too high. This may distort your judgement. Achieving a good balance is easier when you listen critically, at a low volume. Now's the time to make any further adjustments you consider necessary.

The master track

As mentioned at the beginning of this project, our real-life pro audio engineer would be using a professional recording console to record and mix a project such as this. As well as individual channel strips and faders for each track, a recording console has a master section, with its own dedicated master fader. This fader is used to control the overall volume of a mix. The GarageBand equivalent to a recording console's master section is the Master Track. And the GarageBand equivalent to a recording console's master fader can be represented, as a volume curve, on it's own track, on the timeline.

66 From the Track Menu, select Show Master Track (Command-B). The master track will appear complete with a speaker icon. It appears, by default, below the other tracks. Unlike the other tracks, it cannot be moved.

As well as controlling the volume of an entire song, the master track can also be used to transpose complete sections of your tunes. Transposing parts of a song will help add variety to your creations. I'll show you how.

67 Select the newly created Master Track and change the Master Volume curve to Master Pitch.

Info

J ust as you can automate the individual instrument tracks, by inserting control points on the volume curve, so too can you automate the overall master volume of a song. This is useful for creating fade-outs at the end of songs.

68 At bar 29 (after the vocal has finished), insert a control point with a value of +2, on the master pitch curve. Any locked tracks will have to be unlocked first, for this to work.

69 Play the piece through now and everything, except the drums, will sound a tone higher (+2 semitones) at bar 29.
70. We don't have an ending for this project (over to you). After all, it's really only just got underway and there's a lot more that you could do to extend it. For now though place a cycle region from bar 1 to bar 37. When the cycle begins again at bar 1, the tune will return to its original pitch. Your completed project should look something like the next screenshot.

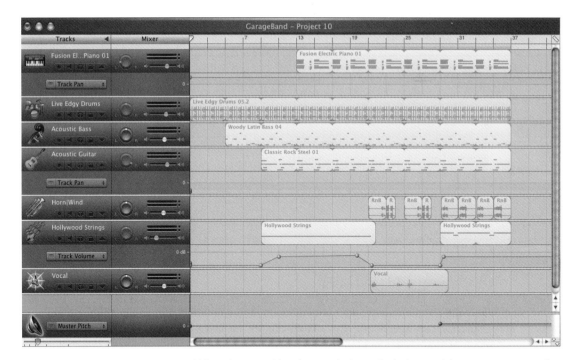

Although everything is now balanced nicely, at this stage our recording engineer would be thinking about how to further polish the mix. The master section on a traditional recording console has facilities to insert signal processors such as compressors, limiters and EQ into the master stereo mix, in the same way that they may have been inserted into the individual instrument and vocal tracks. Only this time, of course, the entire mix is processed. You can do the same in GarageBand.

71 Open the Master Track Info Window (double click the master track). Reverb is already active, of course, because you've already set this, as a send effect.

Although the general levels are fine, I think this track will benefit from some multi-band compression, to smooth out one or two rough edges. Now GarageBand doesn't include a multi-band compressor in its arsenal but OS X does.

72 Activate effects slot 3 and insert the AUMultibandCompressor. You'll find it on the Audio Unit Effects menu. Now, this is a truly wonderful signal processor. However, it's a complicated bit of kit and takes a bit of getting used to. Never mind, choosing any of the presets on offer will bring a distinct audible characteristic to your mix. Try all of them, to hear for yourself. You can experiment and tweak the various parameters afterwards. From my experience though, on this track, the Analog preset works just fine, without the need for too much alteration. So, for now anyway, use that.

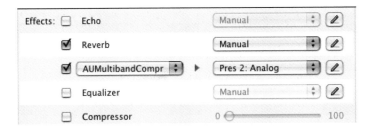

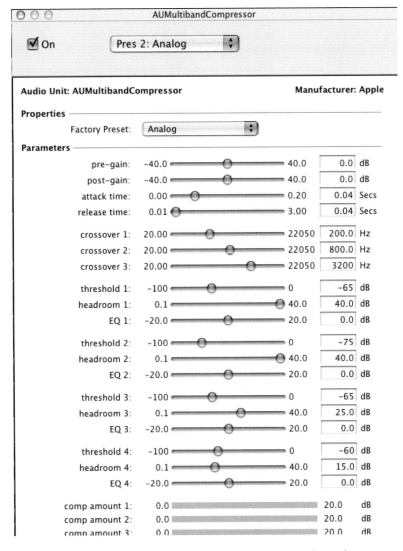

73 When everything is sounding nice and sweet, return to the main GarageBand interface. Check the master track volume level, for signs of clipping. You may not hear anything amiss. However, if the meter hits red, you'll most likely end up with digital distortion if and when you decide to export the mix to iTunes.

That's it; project 10 is complete. You can download my version, for comparison, at http://www.pc-publishing.com/downloads.html.

Assignment

There's a lot more to be done with this project. Find ways to extend it using either new Apple loops or recording material yourself. Apple produce a range expansion packs for GarageBand called Jam Packs. Buy one or two of these and you'll have plenty of loops at your disposal, to continue this project and really make it your own.

Exporting a mix to iTunes

Once you're satisfied with the mix, exporting it to iTunes is simplicity itself.

From the file menu select, guess what?…'Export to iTunes'. Before you do so, check the master level meters. Are they clipping (showing red) at any point in the song? If so, reduce your volume in the master track a little or maybe apply a small amount of compression to the mix. You can now play your song in iTunes along with all the pro stuff you've downloaded at the iTunes music store.

Index

DATE DUE